A Greenpatch Book

Night prowl ers

Written by Jerry Emory
Illustrated by Annie Cannon
with additional drawings
by Renée Menge

Who Is a Greenpatch Kid?

Anyone. Maybe you. All over the world, young people who care about the earth are doing things: helping to save habitats; protecting endangered animals; helping to clean up pollution. If *you* believe that humans need to take better care of the earth, and if you are ready to do your part, you may already be a Greenpatch Kid. For more information about the kids' environmental movement and how you can participate, see page 48.

A Gulliver Green Book
Harcourt Brace & Company
San Diego New York London

Gulliver Green® Books focus on various aspects of ecology and the environment. A portion of the proceeds from the sale of these titles is donated to tree planting projects.

This book is dedicated to Greenpatch Kids everywhere.

Printed in Singapore

Some of the Things in This Book

Greenpatch Kids: Real kids doing real things.
See pages 22, 26, 30, 36, 45.

Where can I find a list of all the animals and projects in this book?
See the index on page 48.

What does that weird word mean?
See the glossary on page 46.

Which nocturnal animals are endangered?
See the list on page 47.

Where can I go to learn more?
See the resources section on page 46.

I want to be a Greenpatch Kid. What do I do?
See the Greenpatch box on page 48.

The Other Half of Every Day

While you were sleeping last night, the world outside your window came to life. Fur-covered legs stretched awake, large eyes blinked open, and sleep-stiff wings flapped in the darkness. Nightshift creatures prepared for *their* day: another evening of running, flying, hunting, and singing under a sky that is thousands of stars deep and countless galaxies wide.

Mother raccoons led their masked infants down the trunks of trees by the light of the moon. Skunks, opossums, ringtails, porcupines, badgers, and kangaroo rats rose from a daytime of rest. Crickets chirped in the neighborhood park, and confused moths fanned the porch light with delicate wings. Lumpy toads hopped from the shadows and croaked into the night air. Moist salamanders wriggled over carpets of leaves, snatching earthworms. An owl swooped down on soft-edged wings from its perch, surprising a field mouse who was busy cutting grass. Coyotes sang moon songs to the sky.

The North Star and its circle of constellations sparkled above. Meteors flashed overhead while a satellite quietly sliced across the sky. Earth raced along its path around the sun at 1,100 miles an hour, while the last light of sunset sped into the darkness of space at 186,000 miles per second!

While you were sleeping, you missed a lot.

Snoozing in the Shadow

sun

Lights in the Shadow as seen by Satellites

A. City lights in Chicago.
B. Oilfields in Algeria burning natural gas.
C. The northern lights (electrical energy from the sun).
D. Sunrise in Egypt. The sunrise will meet Florida, 7,000 miles away, in seven hours.

summer
Earth's orbit
sun
spring
fall
winter

stays light
stays dark
sun's hottest most direct rays
cooler rays hit at a slant
June
December

What is darkness? Darkness arrives when you pass through Earth's shadow. But how is this shadow made? First, some basics on the sun/Earth relationship. Earth is part of the solar system, consisting of a star, our sun, in the center and nine planets that orbit it. Earth is the third closest planet to the sun. Mercury (the closest to the sun) and Venus orbit between Earth and the sun.

Although the sun appears to move across the sky every day, it is actually stationary—we are the ones that are moving!

The planet Earth takes one year (about 365 days) to orbit the sun once. As it travels around the sun, Earth is also spinning like a slow top on its own axis (the North and South Poles). Each rotation on its axis is one day (approximately 24 hours).

Imagine yourself on this slowly rotating Earth at noon—the time of day when your portion of Earth is facing the sun, which is high in the sky. As your portion of Earth begins to turn away from the sun, the sun appears to "set."

When darkness falls each night, your portion of Earth has rotated so that you are temporarily in the shadow on the "backside" of Earth, where the sun's light can't reach. The shadow is *always* there—you just move in and out of it.

Each day and night is one rotation of the planet Earth on its axis, or about 24 hours. But how much of that time is light or dark depends on where you live. If Earth's axis was perpendicular (straight up and down) relative to its path around the sun, then night and day would each be 12 hours long everywhere on Earth, all the time.

But Earth's axis is tilted at exactly 23½ degrees. Along Earth's equator, day and night are always equal, but as you move away from the equator, north or south, days and nights vary in their length and seasonal differences appear. Across the middle of the U.S.—about

40 degrees north of the equator—the longest night lasts about 15 hours (in winter) and the shortest night lasts 9 hours (in summer).

My cousins wrote me from Alaska: "Tuesday Dad bought a new car— but we couldn't really tell what color it was until Saturday. With no school, we were home when the sun finally came up. It was money green (not the sun)."

Hot and Cold

During your wintertime, your portion of Earth is tilted away from the sun, and the sun's rays strike you at an angle. It's cold. In the summer, your portion of Earth is tilted toward the sun so its rays strike you more directly. It's hot.

Far to the north, inside the polar circle, the longest day lasts 24 hours in midsummer and the longest night 24 hours in midwinter. If you lived at the North Pole (0 degrees), darkness and light would last six months each!

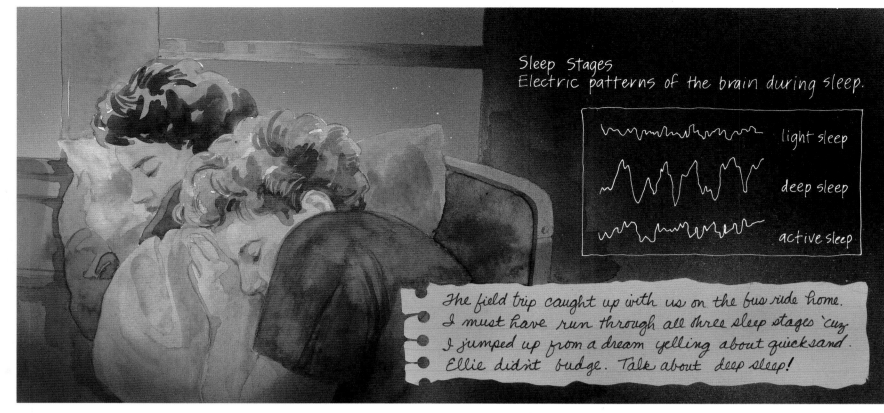

Sleep Stages
Electric patterns of the brain during sleep.

light sleep

deep sleep

active sleep

The field trip caught up with us on the bus ride home. I must have run through all three sleep stages 'cuz I jumped up from a dream yelling about quicksand. Ellie didn't budge. Talk about deep sleep!

A Life Full of Zzzzs

How much do you sleep each night? Five, 10, 15 hours? How much sleep you need to ensure good health depends upon your age. Babies sleep about 18 hours each day. Eight- to 12-year-olds average 10 hours. Teenagers sleep about 8 hours. Grown-ups probably snooze 6 hours. Just imagine, if you live to be 100, you will spend almost 30 years of your life asleep!

The Clock Within

What makes you sleep at night? Maybe someone tells you it's bedtime, but there is something else at work. It's called your *biological clock*. The "clock" is the part of your brain that keeps time on a 24-hour cycle called the *circadian rhythm* (*circadian* is Latin for "about a day"). All living creatures—even plants—have biological clocks.

Sunlight and darkness automatically adjust your clock every day and tell your body when to sleep and when to wake up. People who participate in experiments requiring them to live in caves that are completely shut off from sunlight find their biological clocks begin to malfunction. These cave dwellers may sleep for 18 hours and experience "days" that can last up to 50 hours.

You can confuse your biological clock by staying awake for a couple of days or by flying across the world into another time zone and experiencing jet lag. When this happens, your clock may be off by 6 or 12 hours, and your heartbeat and temperature might become abnormal. You may feel like dancing at midnight and sleeping on your sandwich at noon. After three or four days, your clock will readjust, and you will feel normal again.

Sleeping Potion

Although scientists don't know *exactly* how you sleep, they do know that there is a direct connection between your eyes and your brain's biological clock. When your eyes detect that darkness is coming, they send a message to your brain. Your brain then releases a mixture of *neurotransmitters* into your body. Neurotransmitters are chemicals that carry signals between your nerve cells.

These neurotransmitters are believed to combine to make a "sleeping potion" that makes you feel tired and helps your body relax.

Sleeping in Stages

Once you are asleep, your body goes through certain stages, or levels, of sleep. During the night, your body goes through these different stages about three or four times.

Stage 1: Light sleep

This is when you first fall asleep and your body begins to relax. Some people call this being drowsy. In this stage you will wake up easily if there is a sudden loud noise. Your muscles might twitch gently during this stage, and you might groan one last time before you fall into Stage 2.

Stage 2: Deep sleep

Your body continues to relax during an intermediate period and then settles into deep sleep. During deep sleep, your brain slows down (it takes longer than the rest of your body to relax). Unlike light sleep, this stage is hard to wake from.

Stage 3: Rapid Eye Movement (REM)

Sometimes called "active sleep," REM is characterized by eye movement behind your closed eyelids; your face, fingers, and feet twitch; your breathing and heartbeat change; and more blood flows to your brain. If you watch another person sleep during REM, you are apt to see them wiggle their hands and feet. Your extremities may twitch during REM, but your torso, arms, and legs are "paralyzed." To prevent you from moving around and possibly hurting yourself, your brain doesn't let these larger muscles stir.

Although you can dream at any time during the night, dreams that occur during REM are vivid and wild. REM dreams are also the ones most easily remembered.

Relative size of the planets, in order from the sun.

For their distances from the sun, see page 35.

Sun
870,000

Diameters are given in miles.

Mercury
3,031

Venus
7,521

Earth
7,926

Mars
4,220

Jupiter
88,900

Saturn
74,900

Uranus
31,800

Neptune
30,800

Pluto
1,400

Nightwatch

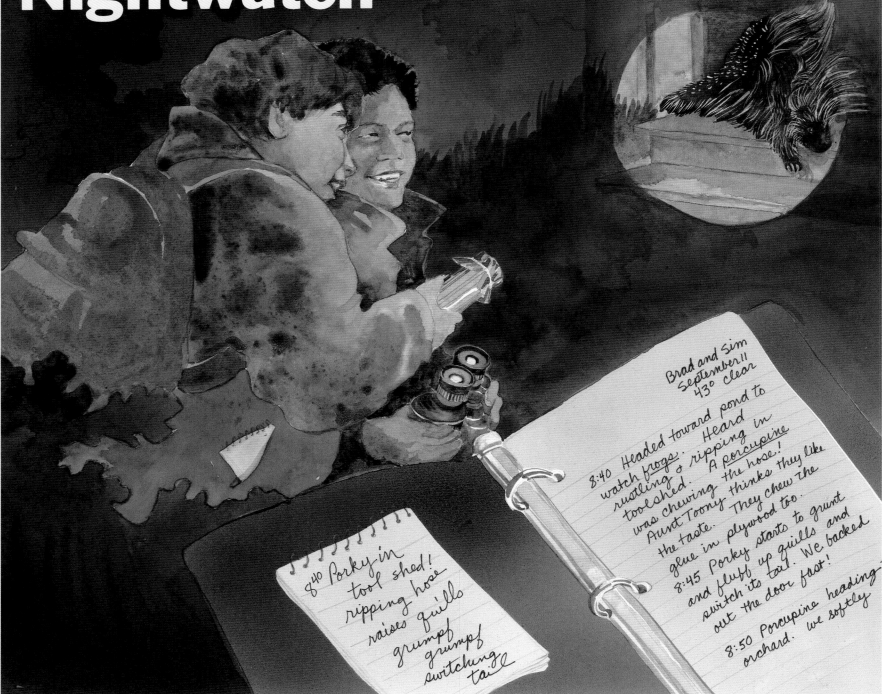

The only way to find out what is going on out there in the dark is to go out and see for yourself. But before you step out to study the stars, observe nocturnal creatures, listen in the dark for night songs, or call an owl, you need to be prepared. To be safe, plan ahead and have the right tools. You have to plan ahead. You need to be safe. And maybe most important, you need to have the right attitude. In many ways, you need to become a night creature yourself: alert, quiet, with all of your senses tuned to the night.

Night Gear

It is important to have the right equipment when nightwatching. Here is some basic gear (add whatever helps you to nightwatch):

1. Flashlight with an attachable red lens (red plastic or cellophane and a rubber band will do). The red light cast by the colored lens will help your eyes adjust to the dark, and it will be less disturbing to night creatures.
2. Binoculars. They bring in a little more light than your eyes and sometimes can help you see better.
3. Watch and compass.
4. Warm clothes and waterproof shoes in winter.
5. Insect repellent in summer.
6. Food and drink (no noisy containers).
7. Small backpack to carry gear.
8. Nightwatch journal (see page 7) and pen or pencil for recording your observations.
9. Camouflaged shelter.

Making Yourself Invisible

When nightwatching, it is best to wear dark clothes so you can blend in with the night. When you rest against a tree trunk or sit quietly in the open, animals will have a hard time seeing you. If you want to cover your scent, rub your camouflage clothes with sage, bay leaves, or any strong-smelling plant. Be very careful anyplace near cars or other vehicles. Your dark clothes will make it hard for drivers to see you.

Night Buddies

Always nightwatch with a friend. Here are a few rules about being a night buddy that will make nightwatching easy and safe:

1. Be sure to tell a grown-up where you are going and for how long.
2. Don't go out without your night buddy. Four ears hear better than two. Two sets of eyes see better than just one.
3. Be ready. Know what you are looking for, what activity you are going to do, and what equipment you need for it.
4. Move carefully and stay together, but don't distract each other with talk. You'll miss too much.
5. Don't pick up anything in the dark unless you're sure what it is.
6. Stargazing is best done when the moon is absent or low in the sky. When the moon is bright, stars are dim.
7. Be home on time.

Build a Nightwatch Shelter

If you and your nightwatch buddy make a simple shelter, you may have better luck observing nocturnal creatures. The idea is to make the two of you as invisible as possible. A shelter is useful only if you set it up near where you expect to see night creatures, so plan the location carefully. You may need to get permission if you put it on someone else's property. Be sure to keep the design simple so you can take your shelter down and move it easily. And be sure to build it so you can see out on at least two sides.

What you need:
frame
large dark blanket or tarp (plastic will rustle
    in the wind and scare away animals)
twine

1. An outdoor table that is big enough for you and a buddy to crawl under makes a great frame for your nightwatch shelter. If you don't have a table outside, use two benches, two patio chairs, two sawhorses, or any two things you can safely put together to make a frame. Place them next to each other but with enough room between them for you and your buddy to sit or lie down.

2. Cover the frame with the blanket, but keep the two ends open for clear observation.

3. Secure the blanket to the frame by tying the corners to the frame with twine. If there are branches or twigs lying around the yard, place them on the shelter to help camouflage it. It doesn't have to hide you 100 percent, just enough so animals won't spot you easily.

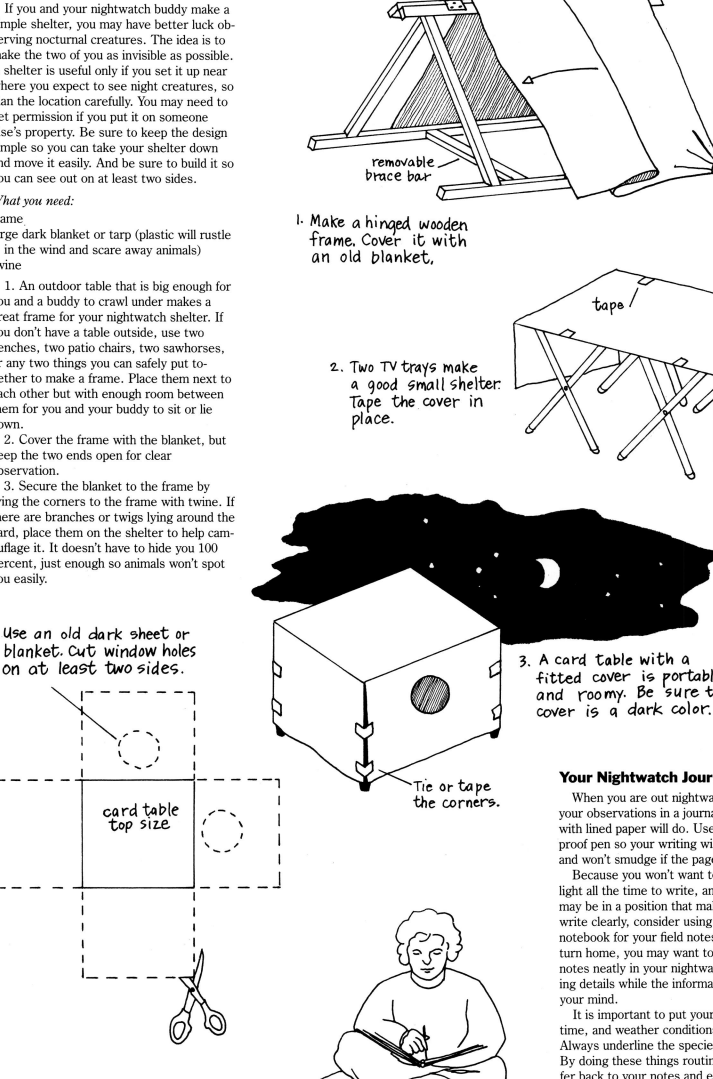

hinge

Tie the corners.

removable brace bar

1. Make a hinged wooden frame. Cover it with an old blanket.

tape

2. Two TV trays make a good small shelter. Tape the cover in place.

3. A card table with a fitted cover is portable and roomy. Be sure the cover is a dark color.

Tie or tape the corners.

Use an old dark sheet or blanket. Cut window holes on at least two sides.

card table top size

Your Nightwatch Journal

When you are out nightwatching, record your observations in a journal. Any binder with lined paper will do. Use a black waterproof pen so your writing will be easy to see and won't smudge if the pages get damp.

Because you won't want to shine your light all the time to write, and because you may be in a position that makes it hard to write clearly, consider using a separate notebook for your field notes. When you return home, you may want to rewrite your notes neatly in your nightwatch journal, adding details while the information is fresh in your mind.

It is important to put your name, the date, time, and weather conditions on each page. Always underline the species you observe. By doing these things routinely you can refer back to your notes and easily compare observations over the years. Also, friends who want to study your notes will find them easy to follow.

Nightwatching Rules

Want to be a nightwatcher? Read these rules and the instructions elsewhere in this book, and follow them carefully. If you do that, you will find the night full of excitement and fascinating adventures. There are two big rules: *be prepared* and *be cautious*.

Be Prepared

Being prepared means being ready for whatever comes along. There is nothing worse than getting drenched because you forgot to bring a raincoat or getting so cold your fingers can't write in your journal. Some of the brightest stars can be seen on the coldest nights. And very interesting things happen at night in the rain. So follow these rules, and you'll have a fine time anyway.

1. Always take a buddy with you. Unless you are nightwatching in your own backyard, never go out at night by yourself.

2. Always tell a grown-up where you are going and how long you expect to be away from home. Don't be upset if your grown-up wants to come along.

3. Know exactly where you are going. Part of getting ready is to visit your nightwatch site in daylight to make plans. What is the safest way to get there? Where will you put your nightwatch station? What will you need to bring? It's good to make a list. How long will it take you to get there, do your nightwatch, and get back? Make your plan, and then stick with it.

4. Ask for permission if you intend to enter or cross private property. Before you complete your plan, be sure to ask for permission. Explain what you are doing. Most property owners will be sympathetic, and they may even have good suggestions.

5. Be equipped. A warm jacket, a flashlight, a wristwatch, your nightwatch journal, and a pencil are essential. Don't leave home without them. There are other items you may want to add, such as a nightwatch shelter, a ground cloth, or other things to make you more comfortable. See this section for more ideas.

Be Cautious

A good nightwatcher moves silently through the night and sits still and watches patiently. If you are careless or crash around in the night, you will not see or hear much.

1. Avoid streets or roadways. If you wear dark clothing to make yourselves "invisible," motorists won't see you either. If you cannot avoid using streets, keep well out of the way of traffic, and use your flashlight as a signal whenever you must cross a street. Better still, wear a white T-shirt over your dark clothing until you are away from traffic.

2. Never venture into unfamiliar territory, even if you think you know your way. Places that looks familiar in daylight may be confusing at night. Keep to your plan.

3. Be silent. One thing you may be sure of: the more noise you make, the less you will see. Work out a set of contact signals with your buddy that will work in the dark without words. Write them down so you will remember, and use them each time so they are familiar. If you must talk, whisper.

4. Be patient. Part of being cautious is being content to sit and wait. This may be the hardest rule for you to follow, but if you do, you will be rewarded. Don't expect too much. Even the smallest night creature has something to teach you. And if you don't see anything the first time out, *don't give up.*

Wild Animals: Look, But Don't Touch

Wild animals are wonderful, and there is no reason to fear them if you are careful. But some animals, even cute ones, can be dangerous. If you are a Greenpatch Kid, you will soon learn how to enjoy nature without risking injury. The best rule is: *look, but don't touch.* Sometimes just the scent of a human is enough to cause a mother animal to abandon her young. Some animal mothers will attack if they think you are a danger. Injured animals are also sometimes aggressive.

Some mammals, such as raccoons, squirrels, bats, and domestic dogs and cats, may carry rabies. Rabies is a serious sickness that can be given to humans through animal bites. If you find a sick or injured animal, or if any animal seems to be acting aggressively, *keep your distance.* Report what you have seen to a grown-up, or call the nearest animal control agency. If you are bitten by an animal, tell a grown-up immediately and see a doctor. *Don't wait.*

If you plan to build a feeding station or shelter for any wild animal, place it away from human or automobile traffic. Think like the animal and choose the kind of location the animal would. Then leave it alone for a while. Wild creatures will not use it until they become used to it, and they may not use it at all if you are always hanging around waiting.

Good wild (or any) animal rules: Be considerate, and always think about the animal's welfare. Look, but do not touch. Be patient.

Dusk

Dusk is a time of change: temperatures drop and winds often stop or start to blow. As the last light fades from the western horizon, and the sky chills from red to dark blue to purple to raven-wing black, stars and planets appear in the night sky.

Daytime animals head for home—a tree, burrow, grassy field, or forest—and night-time creatures begin to stir. Where hawks hovered in sunlight, owls now wing silently. Wide-eyed kangaroo rats replace chipmunks; bats take to the air as daytime birds go to roost.

In the human world, lights are turned on, dogs are called inside, meals are eaten, bathtubs are filled, books are read, and beds are turned down. But wait, there is a lot to learn about the other half of every day. Dusk is simply a warm-up for the night.

Dusk Fliers

After dinner, grandmom took us to the outdoor concert. It started with Mozart. The nighthawks started with peent! peent! peent! At intermission, they all flew back to their roofs. Jeremy thinks some day their feathers will look like the gravel roof instead of like leaves.

whippoorwill

vibrissae

peent! peent!

proboscis

sphinx moth

common nighthawk

white wing bars

As daylight fades, the evening air fills with dusk fliers: bats, nighthawks, moths, mosquitoes, and many other insects. Predators that are active during the day find shelter where they can rest, and dusk fliers take advantage of their absence to search for food and move about. Two common groups of dusk fliers are sphinx moths and goatsuckers.

Goatsuckers

Goatsuckers is the collective name for a unique group of dusk-flying birds in the family Caprimulgidae commonly called nighthawks: the chuck-will's-widow (*Caprimulgus carolinensis*), whippoorwill (*Caprimulgus vociferus*), poorwill (*Phalaenoptilus nuttallii*), and the common nighthawk (*Chordeiles minor*). The name goatsuckers was given to these birds because people once thought they sucked the milk from female goats at night!

Goatsuckers could also be called "soaring insect traps," because they fly slowly through the air with their large mouths open to catch bugs. Long curved facial whiskers, which are called *vibrissae*, help scoop insects into their gaping mouths.

The camouflaged "dead leaf" pattern of goatsucker feathers allows the birds to rest on the ground or lengthwise along a branch during the day and not be seen. Since they lay their eggs on the ground, their patterned feathers help camouflage their nests.

Except for the nasal *peent* call of the nighthawk, all goatsuckers are named for the sound they make. A poorwill's call, for example, is a repetitious whistling *poor-will, poor-will, poor-will.*

Chuck-will's-widows live in the oak-pine woodlands of the southeastern U.S. Whippoorwills range across eastern forests and southwestern mountains. Poorwills prefer the West's dry sagebrush and chaparral country. Nighthawks are common throughout the U.S., both in the countryside and in cities, and they often nest on buildings with flat roofs.

All goatsuckers, except the poorwill, migrate south in the winter. The poorwill crams itself into a rock crevice and hibernates instead. Its breathing slows, and its temperature drops from 102 degrees Fahrenheit to about 65 degrees to save energy. When warm weather returns, it wiggles out and searches for bugs. *Poor-will, poor-will, poor-will.*

Sphinx Moths

There are approximately 120 species of sphinx moths that live in the U.S. They are called sphinx moths because their larvae have a unique way of holding up their heads, like the great Sphinx monument of Egypt.

Sphinx moths range in size from the 2-inch nessus sphinx (*Amphion floridensis*) to the 5½-inch big poplar sphinx (*Pachysphinx modesta*). During the daytime, sphinx moths fold their wings and rest on the shaded branches of trees and plants. At dusk, these fast-flying moths zoom from flower to flower, sipping nectar. They are often called hawkmoths or hummingbird moths, because they dive toward flowers, then hover while they feed.

Sphinx moths are important pollinators of plants. As they sip nectar, they collect pollen on their heads and transfer it to the next flower they visit. Many plants, such as nicotiana, petunia, phlox, trumpet creeper, and honeysuckle, have flowers that are especially adapted to attract sphinx moths. Their flowers are often light colored so the moths can see them in poor light.

As night arrives, many of these same flowers produce powerful scents so sphinx moths can smell their way from plant to plant and continue eating and fertilizing in the dark. Some of the flowers have extended flower tubes so most insects can't reach their nectar. But a sphinx moth has an especially long tubelike tongue called a *proboscis* for drinking nectar. When not in use, the proboscis coils up like a spring. One species of sphinx moth in Madagascar has a proboscis that is 11 inches long!

coiled proboscis

Buggy Visitors

Here are some common nocturnal insects that may be attracted to your porch light or your bug cloth. See how many more you can add to this list on your next nightwatch.

Crane Flies

There are over 1,500 crane fly species in the U.S. Crane flies look like 2-inch mosquitoes, but they aren't related to those biting insects. In fact, crane flies are harmless.

Female crane flies lay hundreds of eggs on the ground or on the marshy shores of ponds. In the spring, the 1- to 1½-inch larvae hatch and either burrow into the ground or float near the edge of ponds. Aquatic larvae have a small facial disk that allows them to keep afloat and breathe. Larvae eat small insects and vegetation. After a few weeks the larvae form cocoons and pupate. About a week later they emerge as adults. Adults live out their short lives either eating small amounts of nectar or nothing at all. They get enough nutrients as larvae to support their adult stage. After breeding and laying eggs, adult crane flies soon die.

Scarab Beetles

There are an estimated 30,000 scarab species worldwide and over 1,000 in the U.S. Scarabs are dark and compact. Many have horns and are ferocious looking, but all are harmless—even the almost 3-inch-long hercules scarab (*Dynastes hercules*) found in the southern parts of the U.S.

Two common scarab species are the tumblebug (*Canthon pilularius*) and the June bug (*Phyllophaga* spp.). The ¾-inch tumblebug lives across the U.S. and is commonly found under animal dung (feces) or dead animals, but it will also crawl toward light. Tumblebugs make little balls out of dung, tumble them into a hole in the ground, and then lay eggs in them.

June bugs alone account for about 130 scarab species in the U.S. These 1½-inch scarabs are best known for their noisy, clumsy flight and their attraction to porch lights.

Green Lacewings

The delicate clear wings and quiet nature of the green lacewing (*Chrysopa carnea*) can be studied on your bug cloth. Adults have small heads, long antennae, and their wingspan averages just under 1½ inches.

The estimated 20 species in the U.S. eat pollen, nectar, and aphid honeydew as adults. As larvae, however, they are voracious predators and chew up aphids with their sicklelike jaws. Lacewing larvae are raised commercially to control aphids in gardens.

Pink-spotted Hawkmoths

The pink-spotted hawkmoth (*Agrius cingulatus*) is one of about 120 species of sphinx moths in the U.S. The pink-spotted has a 4-inch wingspan and is common to most of the U.S. Like many sphinx moths, this species is a strong flier and has even been seen over the ocean, miles from shore.

Their green and pink-dotted larvae are called hornworms, because they have a large horn at the rear of their body. Hornworms eat potato vines and other garden plants.

Polyphemus Moths

The polyphemus moth (*Antheraea polyphemus*) was named after the one-eyed giant of Greek mythology, Polyphemus. It has a large dark eyespot on each wing. The reddish to light brown polyphemus has feathery antennae, a furry body, and a 5-inch wingspan. You will find this moth in most areas of the U.S.

The polyphemus is one of the 65 species of moths in the U.S. that spin their cocoons from silk. Polyphemus cocoons can be found during the fall and winter, hanging from the branches of oak, hickory, elm, maple, and birch trees.

Yellow Woolly Bears

The 2-inch-long yellow woolly bear (*Diacrisia virginica*) is a common U.S. moth. Its color varies from pale yellow to reddish with some small dark spots. The yellow woolly bear gets its name from its furry yellow larva, which has a black head.

The yellow woolly is one of 200 species of moths in the tiger moth family. The larvae of all tiger moths will curl up into balls if you touch them.

Corn Earworm Moths

The pale blue larvae of corn earworm moths (*Heliothis zea*) are the unpleasant surprises you may find as you shuck ears of corn for your summer supper. The adult moths have hairlike antennae, are light brown or yellow, and are covered with dark speckles. They can be found in every state.

Corn earworm moths belong to the Noctuidae family, which includes over 2,700 species in the U.S.

Bugs on a Cloth

Most insects have compound eyes made of many small seeing parts called *facets*. In low light, all facets are open. In bright light, some facets shut down to prevent too much light from entering the eyes.

Moths navigate at night by fixing their position in relation to the moon or bright stars. When they see an unnaturally bright light, like a light bulb, they become confused and fly toward it. This reaction is called *phototaxis*, a word that means turning toward the light.

Do you wonder what kind of flying insects are active at night? Here is a simple way to find out without harming a fly, flea, or moth.

What you need:
white piece of cloth (an old bed sheet will do)
moveable (nonbreakable) lamp
tacks or strong tape
insect guide book
nightwatch journal

Choose a night with little wind and no rain (you'll collect more bugs on a warm night, but it works year-round).

1. Place the lamp next to a window inside your house and turn it on.

2. Go outside and tack or tape the cloth across the face of the window (moths and other nighttime insects can crawl easily on cloth). Now you have a screen that the insects will land on when they "turn toward the light." How many different types of moths and other insects can you count? What are they?

3. Record your findings in your journal.

To help you identify the bugs on your cloth, try your library for these insect guides. Look for the *Golden Guide to Insects, Golden Guide to Butterflies and Moths,* or *The Audubon Society Field Guide to North American Insects and Spiders.*

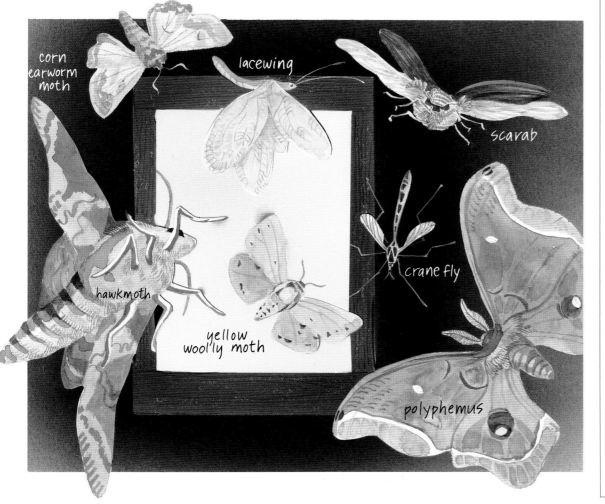

corn earworm moth
lacewing
scarab
hawkmoth
crane fly
yellow woolly moth
polyphemus

Night Songs

Unless you live downtown, you probably think of the night as a quiet time. But in fact, the night is filled with sounds. Tree branches creak as they scrape against each other. Twigs skitter across the pavement and tumble through bushes. Water drips from leaves and gurgles in the distant creek. There are other noises out there. Listen carefully. Who is making all that racket?

Crickets

Perhaps the single most common night sound is produced by crickets. Although crickets can "sing" throughout the year, they are heard most frequently, and most loudly, on warm nights. Only male crickets sing, and they do so by rubbing their wings across one another in a scissorlike motion. Male crickets sing, or rub, to attract females and to defend their territory against other males. To emit a continuous sustained note, some crickets open and close their wings about 40 times per second.

Owls

Whooooooo? The great horned owl (*Bubo virginianus*) booms out the best-known owl call. It's a series of hoots like this: *hoo, hoo-oo, hoo, hoo.* Owls do more than hoot, however. They actually make a wide range of calls. The barred owl (*Strix varia*) sometimes sounds like a barking dog, and the long-eared owl (*Asio otus*) whines like a cat. Saw-whet owls (*Aegolius acadicus*) repeat the same

call—*too-too-too-too*—up to 130 times per minute, and the barn owl's (*Tyto alba*) call is an uninviting hiss. At night, owl calls are the best way to identify the species in your neighborhood.

Foxes

Red and gray foxes (*Vulpes fulva* and *Urocyon cinereoargenteus*) frequently bark at night. Their bark is a raspy, sore-throated sound that jerks their whole body.

Frogs

Both male and female frogs have vocal chords, but in most of these amphibian species only the male calls. Male frogs produce loud and distinctive sounds by pumping air backward and forward over their vocal chords. Frog calls are made louder by balloonlike vocal sacs, which act as amplifiers. Some frogs have only one vocal sac beneath their lower jaw. Others have two smaller sacs that pop out on each side of their head.

Frogs make many kinds of sounds. Some frogs common to the southwestern U.S. sound like they're barking. Large toads are known to cry like human babies, while others even seem to snore. Some tree frogs utter a loud two-part call—*kreck-ek*—about once per second.

Raccoons

A mother raccoon (*Procyon lotor*) makes a low chattering noise to keep her young in tow. But she will snarl, growl, and hiss when confronted by other raccoons, or by your family dog or cat. Raccoons don't always get along with each other. When they fight, they sound like pigs.

Deer

Deer are among the quietest night creatures. These members of the Cervidae family can walk through a forest of dry leaves and fallen branches without making a sound. When alarmed, however, deer let loose an explosive sneeze. Young fawns can sometimes be heard bleating for their mothers. During the breeding season, normally October through December, male deer grunt loudly.

Porcupines

Porcupines (*Erethizon dorsatum*) don't care if they make a lot of noise. Who's going to bother them with all those sharp quills they carry around? When they are not gnawing on tree trunks or fence posts, porcupines can be heard grunting and groaning as they waddle along. When excited they let out a high-pitched cry that is audible a quarter of a mile away.

Coyotes

You have probably heard the distinctive lonely howl of the coyote (*Canis latrans*) in movies about the Wild West, but coyotes actually do their howling all across the U.S. They produce an amazing mix of barks, yips, and howls that can make one coyote sound like a pack of ten. Their vocalization is thought to be one of the ways they communicate with neighboring coyotes. Coyotes are some of North America's most intelligent wild creatures. Their intelligence has enabled them to survive in most parts of the U.S.

Mockingbirds

The mockingbird (*Mimus polyglottos*) produces beautiful melodies that are a mixture of original and imitative songs, each repeated several times. The mockingbird can mimic the sound of just about anything: other birds, squeaky gates, pianos, barking dogs, and much, much more. During the spring, male mockingbirds are known to sing for hours—sometimes they sing all night.

Dogs

No matter where you live, in a city or in the country, you can usually hear a dog barking at night. No one knows for sure why these canines bark. It is known that their hearing is far better than ours, so they might be reacting to sounds we simply can't hear. Of course, dogs also respond to sounds we do hear: other dogs, sirens, fighting cats, and people passing by.

Cats

For the most part, cats are among the quietest nightshift creatures. They only break their silence when they fight or during the mating season. When felines do make noise, however, they don't hold back. Cat screams have been mistaken for crying babies or screaming people.

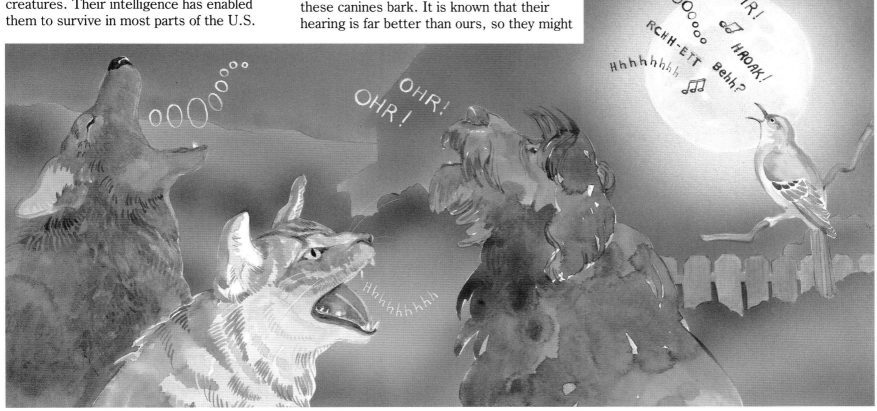

The Listening Post

Learn how to do something wild, nocturnal, and really outrageous: be absolutely quiet for 30 minutes. Sit outside in a comfortable spot *without making a noise* and record everything you hear. *All* night sounds tell you something, and a keen ear is important for all nocturnal naturalists.

What do you hear? A mouse scratching in the leaves? An owl calling in the distance? What is that splashing in the dog's water bowl? Write down what you *think* you hear in your nightwatch journal.

Of course, you aren't always going to hear just the wind or nightshift creatures. You might hear cars, trains, planes, people, or other loud noises. These noises are also part of the natural world, and each one tells some kind of story.

Make a Set of Mouse Ears

Mice can hear *ultrasonic*, or extremely high-pitched, noises made by other mice, as well as the footsteps of predators. If you want to hear better at night, try listening like a mouse.

What you need:
construction paper (thicker than typing paper, thinner than cardboard)
scissors
pencil
stapler or tape

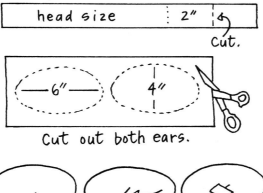

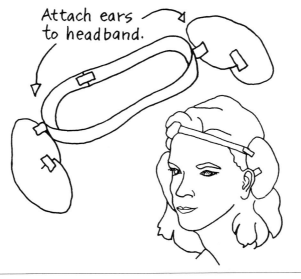

1. Make a 1-inch-by-2-foot paper strip.
2. Use the strip to measure around your head where you would wear a headband. With a pencil, mark where the outside end of the paper crosses the strip. That's how big your head is.
3. Remove the strip from your head and make a second mark 2 inches past your first mark so your strip is as big as your head—plus 2 inches.
4. Cut the strip at the second mark.
5. Bend the strip into a circle until the ends overlap 2 inches.
6. Staple or tape securely. This is your headband.
7. Draw two ovals on another piece of paper, 6 inches long and 4 inches wide. Cut them out. These are your mouse ears.
8. Halfway up the long side of each ear, make a 1-inch cut toward the center.
9. Slide the two cut edges over each other so the ears "cup."
10. Staple or tape where the cut edges overlap.
11. Put your headband on, and mark it 1 inch behind each of your real ears.
12. Remove your headband. Staple or tape the cut side of the ears onto your headband at these marks, so they hang down below the headband, cupped forward, behind your real ears.
Slip on your mouse ears, step outside, and listen like a mouse!

Owls

great horned owl

ear opening behind a ring of face feathers

barn owl

high ear opening

low ear opening

owl skull

Great horned owls hunt mating skunks in February.

Owl babies grow fast and large.

old hawk's nest

What animal can eat a skunk, sleep all day, fly silently in the dark, and turn its head almost completely around without turning its body? The owl, that's *whooo*. Not all owls eat skunks, of course—only the larger ones do. But most owls eat everything from fish and snakes to mice and insects.

There are 20 species of owls in the U.S. They range in height from the 27-inch great gray owl (*Strix nebulosa*) of the northern states, to the 6½-inch elf owl (*Micrathene whitneyi*) of the southwestern deserts. Almost all have dark camouflaged feathers.

Owls have excellent night vision, about ten times better than that of humans. And, unlike most birds, owls have narrow fields of vision because their eyes look forward (most birds have their eyes on the sides of their heads). Owl eyes can't move in their sockets like yours can. To make up for this, owls can do something no other animal can: swivel their heads about 270 degrees without moving their bodies.

Owls also rely on their superior hearing to pinpoint prey in the dark and grab them with powerful talons. To do so they have to fly very quietly so they can listen. Noisy wings would also alert their prey. The secret to the owls' silence is their feathers. Owl feathers are velvety and soft, and the edges of each feather are frayed, which muffles the sound of wings slicing through the air.

Owls sleep during the day in trees and abandoned buildings, and you can sometimes locate snoozing owls by spotting the piles of pellets they regurgitate while resting. At night, owl calls are the best way to identify the species in your neighborhood.

Barn Owl

The 16-inch barn owl (*Tyto alba*) lives across the U.S. and is the species most commonly found living near humans. The barn owl builds nests in hollow trees or on cliff ledges, buildings, and towers. Its diet consists of birds, insects, frogs, and fish. But like all owls, it is also a prolific mouse catcher. The barn owl's white heart-shaped face is unique. The snowy owl (*Nyctea scandiaca*) and the barn owl are the only species that have a lot of white feathers. Barn owls make a raspy, hissing *screeech* call when perched and when flying. Sometimes you can see their white bellies as they wing above streetlamps at night.

Great Horned Owl

The great horned owl (*Bubo virginianus*) and the great gray owl are the two largest owls in North America. The great horned, at 22 inches, is not as tall as the great gray, but it actually weighs more. It weighs 3 to 4 pounds. The "horns" of the great horned owl aren't horns at all, or ears, but tufts of feathers. Although found throughout the U.S., this owl prefers to nest and roost in woods near open areas where the hunting is good.

The great horned is not a picky eater. Small birds, mice, and skunks are common prey. This big owl even has a taste for domestic cats and geese!

The male great horned has a higher voice

When food is scarce, spotted owls may skip a year of nesting.

relaxed tufts

screech owl

spotted owl

raised tufts

squinted eyes

3 cm

Camouflage: with ear tufts raised and round eyes squinted, the screech owl's stripes melt into the bark behind it.

We solved the mystery of the eggshell-in-the-woods with an egg field guide. There aren't many that are round and white, and only the screech owl's was the right size.

than the larger female. The male's call is *hoo, hoo-oo, hoo, hoo,* repeated about four or five times. The female repeats *hoo, hoo-hoo-hoo, hoo-oo, hoo-oo* six or eight times.

Screech Owl

The screech owl lives all across the U.S., in forests, swamps, orchards, deserts, and backyards. With its dark feathers and ear tufts, this 8½-inch owl looks like a miniature great horned owl.

This little owl feeds mainly on mice, voles, and shrews, but it also eats insects. Screech owls will nest in boxes built for them and placed around your home, as will barn owls and saw-whet owls. Screech owl calls include a descending whistle (like a bouncing ball coming to a standstill) and a series of short notes repeated many times. Regardless of its name, it doesn't screech.

The screech owl has recently been classified into an eastern species (*Otus asio*) and a western species (*Otus kennicottii*). Chances are, one or the other of these little owls lives in your neighborhood.

Greenpatch Alert:
Threatened Species
Spotted Owl

This 17-inch owl is so agile it can maneuver between the trees of dense forests in pursuit of small mammals and birds. It nests in hollow trees and is seldom seen unless disturbed. Its call is a series of three or four doglike barks.

The spotted owl (*Strix occidentalis*) is a federally listed threatened species. Throughout its range in the old growth forests of the western U.S., this owl is the center of attention. Loggers want to cut down the trees where the owls live, and environmentalists want to save both the spotted owl and its habitat.

To find out more about the spotted owl and what you can do to help it, write: National Audubon Society, Western Regional Office, 555 Audubon Place, Sacramento, CA 95825. Send a self-addressed, stamped envelope with your letter so it is easier for a representative to write you back.

Owl Pellet Examination

Do you want to find out what your neighborhood owl has been eating? Take a walk in the woods.

Owls eat most of their food whole, because they can't chew (they don't have teeth). Once inside the owl's stomach, mice and other creatures are digested and the leftovers (bones and fur) form a pellet.

The pellet is then coughed up and usually falls to the ground below the perch. Since owls tend to have favorite roosting places, you are apt to find pellets on the ground if you look closely. Try looking anyplace where there are some large trees. Also look for "whitewash" on the ground where owls have defecated while roosting. Pellets dry quickly, don't smell, and are safe to handle (just wash your hands afterward).

What you need:
jar with lid
liquid soap
sieve
tweezers
hand lens
one or more owl pellets

1. Fill the jar halfway with water.
2. Add a drop of soap (this will help break up the pellet).
3. Drop the pellet in the jar and screw on the lid.
4. Shake for 30 seconds.

5. Let the pellet sit in the jar awhile, then shake again.
6. Pour the contents into the sieve over a sink.
7. Take the tweezers and pick the bones and teeth out of the sieve.
8. Arrange on a piece of paper and let dry.

What do you think your neighborhood owl has been eating? Take the hand lens and examine what you find.

Many mammal field guides have sections on skulls and dental patterns that will help you identify what an owl has been eating.

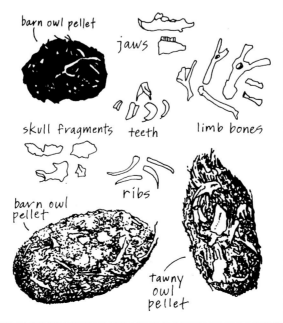

barn owl pellet

jaws

skull fragments

teeth

limb bones

ribs

barn owl pellet

tawny owl pellet

Owl Ears

Owls have amazing hearing. An owl can catch a mouse in complete darkness. Owls have even been observed diving into a field of snow and coming up with a mouse that they heard chewing grass beneath the snow!

Owls' ears are openings on either side of their heads. But unlike your ears, owls' ears don't match. Each is a different size and shape, and in a different position. One is usually round and large. The other is small and slitlike. Each ear is unique, so owls can better detect where sounds are coming from. By turning their heads, owls can more accurately pinpoint noises.

Owls' face feathers form wide dishes behind their ears to help "catch" sounds, just like the exterior parts of your ears do. While perched at night or when hunting in flight, owls are constantly moving their heads back and forth, zeroing in on their prey.

Build an Owl House

You can easily build a house for an owl. Screech, saw-whet, and barn owls commonly nest in such houses.

What you need:
nails and screws
hammer and screwdriver
drill
sandpaper
untreated wood
ladder
grown-up helper

In addition to pieces of wood and nails, you will also need patience. Wild creatures do not hurry to shelters that we build them. Sometimes it takes many months for them to find what we build and to become accustomed to it. So be prepared to wait a long time for visitors. (And don't be surprised if a family of squirrels gets there first.)

1. Your house must fit the owl you wish to attract. Use the table below to choose dimensions. Ask a grown-up to help you cut the wood and assemble the house.

2. Nail the walls to the floor. The roof should be slightly larger than the top of the box to repel rain (if you slope the roof, all the better). The roof should be removable (with screws or small hinges) so you can clean it out each fall after the nesting season. Drill a series of holes and tap out (use a hammer) the round entrance on the front of the box, then sand the edges.

Once your box is completed, wire it securely to a tree trunk or fasten it to the side of a building. Ask a grown-up to help you. Choose a location that doesn't get a lot of human traffic.

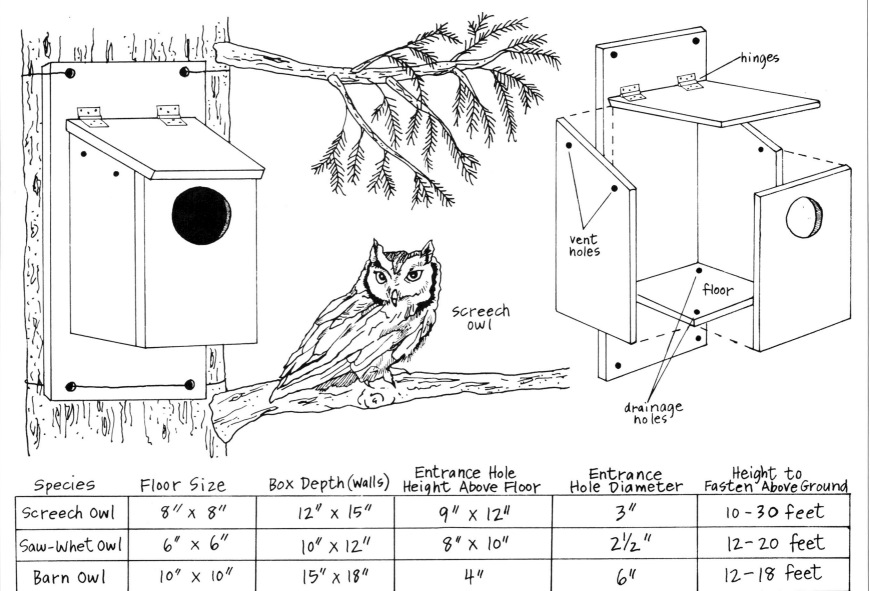

screech owl

hinges
vent holes
floor
drainage holes

Species	Floor Size	Box Depth (Walls)	Entrance Hole Height Above Floor	Entrance Hole Diameter	Height to Fasten Above Ground
Screech Owl	8" x 8"	12" x 15"	9" x 12"	3"	10 - 30 feet
Saw-Whet Owl	6" x 6"	10" x 12"	8" x 10"	2½"	12 - 20 feet
Barn Owl	10" x 10"	15" x 18"	4"	6"	12 - 18 feet

Give a Hoot

Owls are very territorial. If you learn how to call like the owls living near you, they will fly toward you and answer back. The great horned owl call is a good one to begin with because it is pretty easy to imitate. The male sounds like this: *hoo, hoo-oo, hoo, hoo,* repeated about four or five times. Cup your hands over your mouth. With a little practice, you'll sound like a great horned owl.

To learn owl calls go outside at night and listen, or ask your library if it has a bird call record or video you can practice with. Now go outside and try your owl calls. Stop and listen. Repeat. Any answers?

Ask if your library has *A Field Guide to Bird Songs, The Peterson Field Guide Series* (record, Western and Eastern U.S. editions), or *Audubon Society's Videoguide to the Birds of North America.*

American Owls

NAME	RANGE
(T) = Threatened	
Barn Owl	Entire U.S.
Tyto alba	
Eastern Screech Owl	Eastern States
Otus asio	
Western Screech Owl	Western States
Otus kennicottii	
Whiskered Screech Owl	Southern Arizona
Otus trichopsis	
Flammulated Owl	Western States
Otus flammeolus	
Great Horned Owl	Entire U.S.
Bubo virginianus	
Snowy Owl	Northern States
Nyctea scandiaca	
Northern Hawk Owl	Northern States
Surnia ulula	
Northern Pygmy Owl	Western States
Glaucidium gnoma	

NAME	RANGE
Ferruginous Pygmy Owl	Southern Arizona
Glaucidium brasilianum	
Elf Owl	Arizona, New Mexico, Texas
Micrathene whitneyi	
Burrowing Owl	Midwest and Western States
Athene cunicularia	
Barred Owl	Midwest and Eastern States
Strix varia	
Spotted Owl (T)	Pacific Coast and Southwest
Strix occidentalis	
Great Gray Owl	Pacific Northwest
Strix nebulosa	
Long-eared Owl	Entire U.S.
Asio otus	
Short-eared Owl	Entire U.S.
Asio flammeus	
Boreal Owl	Northern U.S.
Aegolius funereus	
Northern Saw-whet Owl	Entire U.S.
Aegolius acadicus	

Night Senses

eyeshine from a flying squirrel's tapeta

rods and cones

tapeta

light bouncing off tapeta, hitting rods twice

A cat's pupils will close to slits for daytime hunting.

as seen by human eyes

as seen by a moth with ultraviolet vision

dark lines point to the nectar

evening primrose

Like most humans you understand your world mainly through what you see. Certainly you can hear, feel, and smell, but for most people, to see is to understand. That's why we often say, "See what I mean?" Many nocturnal creatures understand the world just as well—if not better—than we do. They get around at night using various highly developed senses. So if they could talk, night animals might say, "Feel what I mean?" or "Smell what I mean?" On a moonless night you may not be able to see anything when you go outside, but for many creatures that same night is full of light. What is the difference between your eyes and theirs?

Night Eyes

Except for insects and their unique compound eyes, all animal eyes are lined with *rods* and *cones*. Cones examine detail; rods absorb light. Because you are *diurnal* (active in daylight), your eyes have more cones than rods. Diurnal eyes are able to distinguish small details very clearly, but only if there is plenty of light.

The eyes of nocturnal animals are packed with rods and have only a few cones. Nocturnal eyes do not distinguish small details, but they are able to detect shapes and movement in dim light. Also, some animals can see forms of light that you can't. Birds that migrate at night can see *polarized light*, and nocturnal insects see *ultraviolet light*.

Many night creatures have dual purpose eyes; they are able to see during the day and night. To see well at night these animals have shiny membranes called *tapeta* behind their rods and cones. At night the tapeta reflect weak light back through the eye. By using light twice, the animal can see better.

Eyeshine

When light from your flashlight or car headlight shines in the eyes of an animal with tapeta, the color of light reflected back varies according to the species. How many night creatures can you identify by their eyeshine?

white	Fox
yellow	Raccoon
amber	Skunk
dull orange	Opossum
red-orange	Flying Squirrel
red	Black-tailed Jackrabbit
deep red	Porcupine
yellow	Deer
green-gold	Coyote/Mountain Lion
green	Domestic Cat and Dog

Snake Eyes

To protect their light-sensitive eyes, many night creatures have eyes equipped with vertical (up and down) pupils that can close to small slits during the day. This is how they prevent too much light from coming into their eyes and "blinding" them (especially if they are disturbed during the day and have to move about).

Your pupils are round so they can absorb as much light as possible. But cats, crocodiles, geckos, lizards, and snakes all have vertical slits in their eyes. Scientists aren't sure why, but certain species, like some frogs and toads, have horizontal (sideways) pupils.

Night Vision Tests

When you go outside at night, you don't see very well at first. Why not? Try this: when you venture out, find a comfortable place to stand or sit and close your eyes for a couple of minutes. When you open them, you'll be able to see better.

Go outside at night with a buddy (let's call him or her Sam), and bring a flashlight. Face Sam and stand about a foot away. Turn the flashlight on and hold it down by your side so the light hits the ground. Look directly into Sam's eyes, then slowly bring the light close to Sam's eyes but don't shine it straight at them. Move it away, then repeat. What happens to Sam's pupils?

While you and Sam are out checking your night vision, here is something else to try. Ask Sam to stand about 50 feet away from you. Looking directly at Sam, ask him/her to wave at you. Now, look away slightly and ask Sam to wave again. Is there a difference?

There should be. You are able to detect movement in the dark much better out of the corners of your eyes because you have more rods at the edge of your field of vision and fewer cones. So if you think you see something straight ahead, look to the right or left. If whatever it is moves, you'll probably see it.

Fur, Feathers, and Whiskers

Fur on mammals and feathers on birds help protect them, but they also help them feel their way in the dark. Each hair, and every feather, is attached to a network of nerves. When the hairs and feathers move, a message is sent to the nervous system, which translates and interprets that movement.

In mammals and some birds, whiskers called *vibrissae* are sensitive feeling organs. In mammals, they grow along the belly, legs, and, especially, the face. Cat whiskers are vibrissae. Owls and goatsuckers also have vibrissae on their faces. Goatsuckers use their vibrissae to detect and scoop up insects. They might also help protect the birds' eyes. Vibrissae are highly sensitive to air movement and may tell mammals when other animals are nearby.

Antennae

The antennae of insects are similar to vibrissae. They, too, are highly sensitive touching organs. Not all antennae are located on heads. Some insects and spiders have long legs that act like antennae. Earthworms have small antennae all over their bodies. Cockroaches have two short spikes on the rear of their bellies that feel air movements. When the spikes detect motion, the cockroach begins to run away within 1/20 of a second!

Many species, like crickets and spiders, feel *and* smell with their antennae. Snails smell with their antennae and the edges of their feet. Snakes don't have antennae, but they flick out their tongues, scoop up chemical particles (smells), flick them into a special smelling organ on the roofs of their mouths, and interpret them.

Smell and Taste

Your nose and mouth are lined with cells called *chemoreceptors* that are sensitive to the microscopic chemical molecules in smells and food. Your senses of smell and taste are very similar, but the receptors in your nose are 3,000 times more sensitive than the ones in your mouth! Food has to be in your mouth for you to taste it. Your nose can detect faint smells from far away.

When your nose detects airborne molecules, it sends a message to your brain. Your brain then translates that message: "Aha! Apple pie!"

Most insects and animals have far better senses of smell and taste than you do. A salmon can return to the freshwater stream where it hatched by following the "smells" found only in that stream. Many nocturnal mammals, such as deer, bears, rabbits, and badgers, not only have more powerful noses than you do, but they leave scent trails to mark their territories and to help them find their way.

Some animals produce scents from their glands, and to mark their territory, they rub their scent onto branches and rocks or leave their scent on the ground when they urinate or defecate. Male moths have enormous antennae that they use to detect the scent produced by the female of their species. These antennae may have up to 1,700 tiny hairs that capture scent molecules, allowing the male to follow a female from a mile away.

Vibrissae protect a deer's eyes.

We think it's a male beetle from its antennae. It spreads the branching parts apart, like fingers on a spaghetti server. Then it squeezes them flat shut when we open a vanilla bottle near it.

scent gland

shoulder scent gland

scent gland under chin

deer hoof

kangaroo rat

rabbit "chinning"

Scent Trails

A fox rubs saliva on vegetation.

Dark

From the time you wriggle into bed and pull your covers up around your neck, to when you are deep in REM sleep at midnight, the Big Dipper will have rotated 90 degrees around the North Star. The moon will have floated five hand-spans across the night sky.

It's "high noon" on the nightshift. Raccoons frisk shoreline rocks and marsh grass, probing for snappy crawfish and tasty, moist frogs. Deer pause, tense and alert. They twitch, sniff, and listen for sounds that hint of danger.

It's a wild world under this cover of darkness; just ask your cat in the morning how many mice got away from her in the vacant lot next door, or how slimy that salamander was that she couldn't resist playing with. Eyes, ears, and antennae are on full alert outside your window right now. The night is alive with possibilities.

Bats

mouth open, emitting clicks that echo off insects

little brown bat hunting mosquitoes

range of little brown bat

bat's thumb and fingers

pallid bat munching scorpion

range of pallid bat

Vampire bat in Mexico feeding from wound on sleeping burro.

Bats have been hanging around for about 50 million years and are among the earth's oldest animals; they are also some of the most misunderstood. Because they are nocturnal and strange looking, people have associated bats with evil things—such as Count Dracula and witches—for centuries. Nothing could be further from the truth. In fact, bats play very important economic and ecological roles in the world.

In rain forests and deserts, bats are some of the most important pollinators of plants. Without bat pollinators, the wild varieties of many foods you eat—avocados, bananas, cashews, mangoes, and peaches—couldn't grow! And as natural insect controls, they can't be beat. One colony of bats studied in Florida ate some 50 tons of insects every year, including over 15 tons of mosquitoes!

There are nearly 1,000 species of bats worldwide, most of which live in tropical regions. Forty-three species live in the U.S. In fact, almost a quarter of the world's mammals are bats. Bats are the only mammal that can fly and are in a special order called Chiroptera, which means "hand-wing." Bats' wings are actually membranes of skin stretched between their hands and their legs. Like humans, bats are communal creatures. They live in groups. They give birth to helpless young and are fed breast milk by their mothers. Although often thought of as "flying mice," bats are actually more closely related to primates (that's you!).

Little Brown Bat

The little brown bat (*Myotis lucifugus*) is the most common bat in the U.S. It can be found in empty parts of buildings, although caves, abandoned mines, and tree hollows are also favorite roosts. With a wingspan of just over 9 inches, the little brown bat can zoom around and catch up to 600 insects in one hour. Its healthy appetite for insects, mostly mosquitoes, proves how beneficial to humans a little brown bat can be.

Pallid Bat

The pallid bat (*Antrozous pallidus*) lives along the Pacific Coast, throughout the southwestern U.S., and Mexico. With its 15-inch wingspan, enormous ears, and pale yellow coloration, the pallid bat is a striking sight. If you see one, you won't mistake it for anything else.

Unlike most bats, the pallid feeds mostly on the ground, eating crickets, beetles, and scorpions. It is believed that the hearing of pallid bats is so sensitive that they can hear the footsteps of approaching scorpions.

Mexican Free-tailed Bat

Because about a third of this bat's tail sticks out beyond its rear membrane, it is

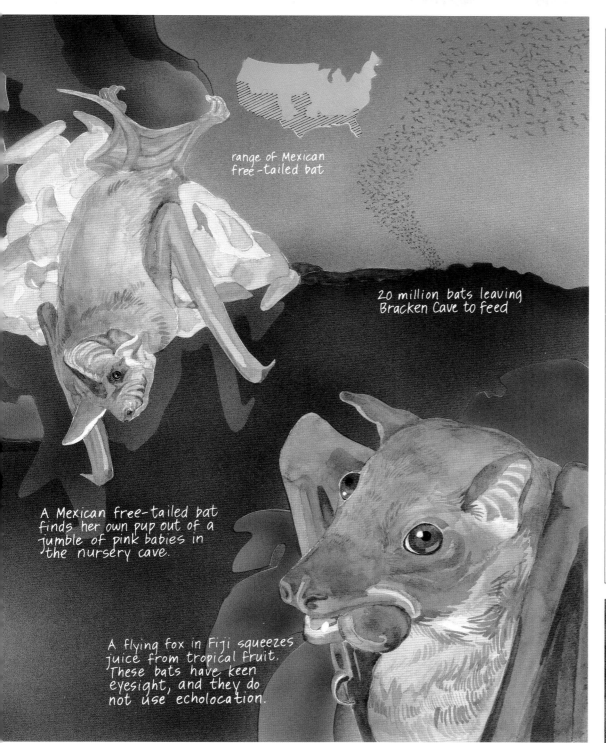

range of Mexican free-tailed bat

20 million bats leaving Bracken Cave to feed

A Mexican free-tailed bat finds her own pup out of a jumble of pink babies in the nursery cave.

A flying fox in Fiji squeezes juice from tropical fruit. These bats have keen eyesight, and they do not use echolocation.

Greenpatch Alert:
Endangered Bat Species

Bats are endangered worldwide. Seventeen of the 43 U.S. species are recognized by bat experts as endangered, though only six bats are officially listed as endangered by the federal government: lesser long-nosed (*Leptonycteris curasoae*), gray (*Myotis grisescens*), Indiana (*Myotis sodalis*), Hawaiian hoary (*Lasiurus cinereus semotus*), Ozark big-eared (*Plecotus townsendi ingens*), and Virginia big-eared (*Plecotus townsendi virginianus*).

The reason why so many species are endangered is because humans disturb the places where bats roost, hibernate, and raise their young. These places are often caves. The six endangered species listed above spend at least half of their lives in caves. For example, the gray bat population dropped 80 percent in recent decades due to vandalism in their hibernation caves in the central and southeastern states. Thanks to conservation efforts, the gray bat population is rebounding. Other reasons for decline include contamination from pesticides and habitat destruction, which reduce the insects and plants that feed bats.

To find out more about bats, and what you can do to help them, write: Bat Conservation International, P.O. Box 162603; Austin, TX 78716-2603. Send a self-addressed, stamped envelope with your letter so it is easier for a representative to write you back.

This small bat cave entrance is protected by a grate. Bars let bats fly in and out and keep vandals out.

named "free-tailed." Tails of other bats are encased in the membrane stretched between their hands and feet. The entire population of Mexican free-tailed bats (*Tadarida brasiliensis*) lives in only 12 known caves.

The Bracken Cave, located near New Braunfels, Texas, is shelter for more than 20 million bats. When the bats leave the cave to feed at dusk, they form a trail almost 2 miles long. It is estimated that the Bracken Cave population alone consumes 250,000 pounds of insects each night!

Flying Foxes

Flying foxes, members of the Megachiroptera order, aren't foxes at all. They are the world's largest bats. They live in Southeast Asia and on islands across the Pacific and Indian oceans. The wingspan of some flying fox species is more than 6 feet across. These bats eat mostly fruit and are hunted for food (in some places they are considered a delicacy!).

Blood Suckers

Many people are scared to death of bats, especially vampire bats. Relax. There are only three species of vampire bats, and all live in Latin America.

Vampire bats make tiny scrapes on the skin of sleeping mammals, which they cover with an anticoagulant that prevents the blood from clotting. Then they lap up the dripping blood, which is rich in protein. Despite what you may think, *no* bat species deliberately attacks humans. But, for a vampire bat, a sleeping human is just another sleeping mammal.

In many parts of Asia and China, bats are respected. The flying foxes of some Pacific Islands are heroes in legends, and the Chinese believe bats signify good luck and happiness. It is only in Europe and the U.S. that bats are feared and persecuted, and their true nature is clouded by myth, superstition, and misunderstanding.

Echolocation

Bats catch the smallest night-flying insects with the greatest of ease. How? By *echolocation*. Perched or flying, bats emit a series of extremely high-pitched squeaks or clicks, some of which you can hear. When perched, they produce about 10 clicks per second, but while flying and chasing insects this increases to about 200 clicks per second.

These clicks bounce off of objects (as small as a human hair) and are heard by the bat when the echo returns. This way bats can

calculate how far away objects are and can "see" in total darkness. "Blind as a bat" is a common saying, but it isn't true. Most bats can see just fine with their eyes, but their ability to "see" by echolocation is far superior.

Test a Bat

Here is a simple game you can play with bats, especially on your next summer camping trip. If you see some bats at dusk flying low over an open area, you can get their attention with a handful of small pebbles.

When you see a bat approaching, toss a pebble into the air several yards in front of the bat. Be careful not to hit the bat. The bat will detect the rock, drop down while bombarding it with sound waves, then pull up when it "sees" that it is a pebble and not a tasty mosquito.

Build a Bat House

Bats are endangered worldwide because their habitats are destroyed or disturbed by humans. You can build a bat house and help save the bats in your neighborhood. Here is a small-sized box that could be home for as many as 30 little brown bats. Like any other wild creatures, bats may not use your shelter right away. Be patient. It might take weeks or even months before your bat neighbors decide to move in. Watch for them just before dark.

What you need:

hammer and nails
½-inch-thick wood (untreated): back piece = 12 inches wide and 27 inches long; front piece = 12 inches wide and 22 inches long; two side pieces = 3 inches wide and 22 inches long; roof = 14 inches by 6 inches; inside strip of wood = 12 inches long and 1¼ by 2 inches
grown-up helper

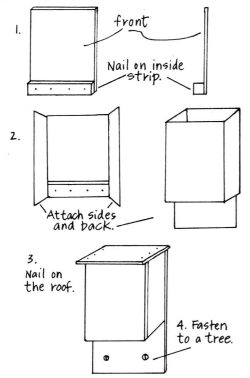

1. For the bats' entrance, nail the 1¼-by-2-inch strip to the front piece, so it is flush with the bottom and sides of the front piece (easiest to attach before nailing the box together).

2. Attach the sides to the front, then attach the back piece, keeping them all flush on top. There will be a slot left open on the bottom about 1 inch wide, where the bats enter.

3. Nail on the roof so it is flush with the back piece. It will hang over the front and side pieces. It is very important that the inside surface of all the boards be rough wood, or cut with horizontal grooves at ½-inch intervals, so the bats can hang on with their small sharp claws.

4. Your bat house can be attached in a variety of ways, depending on where it is hung. Use either nails, screws, hooks, or brackets, and check the house occasionally to make sure it is firmly attached. Fasten it to a tree at least 10 to 15 feet above the ground. Try to place it away from human or vehicle traffic. If possible, face it east or southeast so it can warm in the morning sun. Make sure no branches block the entrance.

Greenpatch Kid

Bats Were on His Mind

Bert Grantges may be thinking about college right now, but 13 years ago, bats were on his mind. "I don't remember exactly when I started liking bats. I guess I was about four or five years old. I do remember looking through a book with some great pictures. I got my mom and dad to read to me what the pictures were about. The book was all about bats. Ever since I've been really interested in bats."

After he first discovered bats, Bert was soon looking at and eventually reading everything he could about them. When he was ten years old, he met bat researcher Dr. Merlin Tuttle, who had just moved his organization, Bat Conservation International, from Wisconsin to near Bert's home in Austin, Texas. Bert impressed Dr. Tuttle with his ability to identify all the bats pictured on Dr. Tuttle's office walls.

Their meeting changed Bert's life. "Gosh, ever since then, I've been traveling around the world with him, to Mexico, Costa Rica, and Australia, conducting research and studies."

The first big trip Bert took with Dr. Tuttle was to Texas's Bracken Cave to look for Mexican free-tailed bats. Bert spent part of that summer near Big Bend, Texas, looking for spotted bats. "We went down there three times and never found that bat. But the first trip was great. The first two nights there we caught over 600 bats representing 14 different species. Fantastic!"

Bert quickly learned how to wear gloves, headlamps, and use mist nets and bat bags (to hold captured bats). "Bat biologists use the word *netting* a lot. Like, 'I'm going out netting tonight.' Because that is how we catch bats, in mist nets. We usually set up the net near some water and when it is still light. Then we rest and come back when it is dark. Because different bats are active at different times of the night, on a good night you can catch bats all night long. They get caught in the net as they fly around, then we carefully untangle them, study and measure them, and let them go."

Before Bert goes off to college, he is spending the summer conducting research on the threatened bats of Arizona. He will use small radio transmitters attached to the bats to find out where they eat and sleep. "When I get that information," says Bert, "it will be easier to know what areas should be protected to help these bats."

Beastly Nights

Who is up when you are down? An amazing number of creatures are out and about at night. Here are just a few of the more common ones you might see. How many of these nocturnal creatures visit your neighborhood? One good way to find out is to plan a night or two each month for nocturnal observations. Get permission to stay up late (or get up early) and record what you see in your nightwatch journal. Do this for a whole year, and you'll have a pretty good idea who roams your neighborhood at night. Be patient. It may take you some time to get used to nightwatching. But even if you live in a city or suburb, you'll be amazed at what's out there.

Raccoons

Whether you live in a big city, a small town, or the country, raccoons (*Procyon lotor*) live there too. They are the most curious nocturnal animals you'll see. They have distinctive black "bandit" masks across their eyes and thick, black-and-white ringed tails. Adults weigh up to 35 pounds, or about as much as a medium-sized dog. Their long-fingered front paws look like miniature versions of your hands, and they are capable of opening outdoor cabinets. They can even pop can tops with ease. The name raccoon comes from the Algonquian Indian language, and it means "he scratches with his hands."

These night creatures live everywhere in the U.S., except the high western mountains. They nest in hollow trees in the country and sometimes in storm drains in the city. Two similar-looking species related to raccoons are restricted to the Southwest: the ringtail (*Bassariscus astutus*), which is smaller and lacks the bandit mask; and the coati (*Nasua narica*), which has a longer, skinnier tail and a long nose.

Raccoons are *omnivorous*. That means they eat anything they want. Around town or in a park, you sometimes see their tails sticking out of dumpsters. They might steal food from your dog's bowl at 2 A.M. or scoop goldfish from your neighbor's pond. They also love to raid gardens, dig for worms, or eat corn. In the country, raccoons prefer frogs, bird eggs, and insects, and they can be found around water, where they frequently wash their food. Mounds of neatly cleaned clam and mussel shells will tell you that raccoons visited a stream or marsh last night.

In the spring, mother raccoons can give birth to seven young, but litters average about four. Baby raccoons are blind at birth, but within four to five weeks they can see, and after about two months they venture forth each night with their mothers.

Raccoons are very vocal, and mothers chatter constantly to keep their children in line. During the mating season, or when they are fighting, raccoons growl and snarl loudly.

Raccoon Central

Some people keep raccoons and other wildlife as pets or feed them on their porch. As cute as they are, you must remember raccoons are wild animals. Instead of inviting them to be houseguests, make a place for them to eat in a corner of your yard.

Place a board (6 by 12 inches will do) or an old bowl on the ground or in a tree where you can leave food scraps, such as vegetables, meat, or bread. A water bowl would also be good. If there is an outside light that illuminates the scene, leave it on. The raccoons will become accustomed to it, and you'll be able to watch them with binoculars. You may be surprised at how many other night creatures will visit raccoon central. Be patient. It may take several weeks before they decide raccoon central is safe.

claw holes

front track

Long claws help skunks rip up logs to find ants.

Striped Skunks

Striped skunks (*Mephitis mephitis*) are about the size of house cats, but with a *powerful* difference: they can spray a repulsive odor from their rear-end scent glands when attacked. *Mephitis* is Latin for "a foul odor."

A striped skunk is all black with a bold white stripe that runs from its nose down its back to the tip of its large fluffy tail. Stripeds are very common and live in every state in the U.S., both in the country and in cities. Three other skunk species also live in the U.S. The hooded skunk (*Mephitis macroura*) and the hog-nosed skunk (*Conepatus mesoleucus*) live only in the Southwest. The spotted skunk (*Spilogale putorius*) lives everywhere except the far northern states.

Skunks are members of the Mustelidae family, which includes weasels, ferrets, otters, wolverines, and badgers; all of which have scent glands. Only skunks can spray their offensive aroma, but they don't let loose at random. Their black-and-white coloration is a warning signal in the animal world. If animals, or you, don't heed the warning, a skunk will face the enemy, raise its tail, and arch its back to show off its black-and-white signal. Next it will stamp the ground with its front feet, shuffling backward between stamps. If *this* warning doesn't work, it will twist its rump toward the enemy and spray.

The powerful stuff skunks spray is musk, an oily liquid produced in two grape-sized glands below their tails. Muscles squeeze the glands so forcefully that skunks can shoot up to 15 feet with great accuracy. Musk is so powerful it can temporarily blind you, make you throw up, or cause a rash. It even knocks some animals unconscious.

Not surprisingly, skunks don't have many natural predators. However, great horned owls eat skunks because the owls don't have much sense of smell.

Stripeds are omnivorous and active all night looking for mice, insects, and berries. They burrow under buildings or rock mounds, where they spend the winter sleeping. It isn't true hibernation, because they wake up and roam around if the weather warms. When spring arrives, females give birth to between five and ten young, called kits. When the kits are three weeks old, they can begin to spray, and after a few months when they follow their mother in a single file during her nocturnal ramblings, they are fully armed.

Cottontails

The eastern cottontail (*Sylvilagus floridanus*) lives across most of the U.S. and is typical of the eight cottontail species in this country. This 4-pound rabbit with 3-inch ears lives in brushy and wooded areas, where it is active from early evening to late morning. It eats green vegetation during the summer and chews on twigs and bark during the winter. During the day, it rests under bushes or in burrows.

All cottontails have gray fur and white tails that flash when they hop and run. The exception is the New England cottontail (*Sylvilagus transitionalis*) with its reddish summertime fur and white-flecked winter coat. All have similar eating habits and are considered garden pests because they love fresh green plants.

Although cottontails look defenseless and cute, when cornered they can kick predators (bobcats and raccoons) in the face with their powerful legs and sharp nails.

Cottontails give birth to between two and six young in the spring or summer. Cottontail mothers place their young, who are blind for a few days, in fur-lined nests when they leave to eat. They return frequently to nurse their young. Within a week, the young cottontails have their eyes open and can see.

Deer

Two of the deer species that live in the U.S. are white-tailed deer (*Odocoileus virginianus*) and mule deer (*Odocoileus hemionus*). White-tailed deer live across the entire country, except for some western states. Mule deer live in the western half of the country. This means both species live side by side in many central and some western states.

Both have reddish brown or gray fur in summer and thick blue-gray coats in winter. Adult males weigh up to 400 pounds, and females grow to between 50 and 200 pounds. Deer can run as fast as 40 miles per hour and jump 30 feet horizontally.

The major difference between these species is that the white-tailed deer does, in fact, have a tail that is white on its underside. When frightened, it lifts its tail in the air like a flag and bounds away. The mule deer has larger ears than the white-tailed deer and a black-tipped tail that it holds down when running.

Deer are usually very quiet, but when alarmed they sneeze loudly. During the winter mating season, called the *rut*, male deer grunt loudly defending their small herd of females. In the spring, fawns can be heard bleating for their mothers.

Male deer grow antlers every spring. The older the male, the bigger the rack of antlers. The American record for antler size is 47½ inches from tip to tip. When they first grow, antlers are covered with a soft furlike coating called *velvet*. Males constantly rub their antlers against tree trunks and bushes to remove the velvet. These scrapings can be seen on tree trunks everywhere. By the rut, their antlers are velvet free and sharp so males can battle each other over females. After rut, antlers drop off in late winter and can be found on the ground.

We put the bunnies back where we found them and marked their nest with a yarn "x," like the wildlife people said. Kevin kept his water pistol ready for cats.
Sure enough, the mother rabbit came back. She hadn't abandoned them after all.

The deer's raised tail alerts the rest of the herd to danger.

Surviving a Hard Winter

Sunk in mud at the bottom of iced-over ponds, bullfrogs hibernate.

By absorbing air from the water through their skins, they 'do not drown'.

2½"

Coyotes listen for mice scurrying through air pockets beneath the snow... then pounce.

Coyotes

The coyote (*Canis latrans*) lives across the U.S., mostly in the countryside. But as people build more houses near wild areas, coyotes are becoming backyard "pests." The adaptable coyote has even been seen on the outskirts of large southwestern cities and near downtown Los Angeles.

The coyote's scientific name means "barking dog." On still nights, coyotes can be heard yipping, barking, and howling across open meadows, deserts, and in wooded areas. One coyote can make so much noise it is apt to sound like a whole pack. Coyotes weigh as much as 50 pounds, though most are lighter. They are gray or reddish gray, and have rust-colored legs, feet, and ears. At a distance they look like medium-sized domestic dogs, but can be distinguished by their bushy tails, which they hold down when running.

Like most dog species, coyotes are social and often hunt in pairs. During a typical night of hunting, they can cover 10 miles. Some coyotes have been tracked more than 100 miles in a single night!

During the April to May pupping season, females retreat to an underground den or a small cave and give birth to between five and ten young. After about two weeks, the pups' eyes open, and soon they are wrestling with each other and pestering their mother for food.

Coyotes eat mice and rabbits and, in fact, help farmers by keeping these animals under control.

Unfortunately, they are killed in this country by government hunters working for the Animal Damage Control Program because they occasionally kill domestic livestock. Recent studies, however, have shown that much of the livestock believed to have been killed by coyotes was actually chased down by packs of domestic dogs.

In Native American mythology, coyotes are often portrayed as tricksters, able to outsmart fellow animals and humans. That's because they really are one of the smartest and most adaptable animals in the world.

Bullfrogs

Bullfrogs (*Rana catesbeiana*) are the largest species of frog in the U.S.—over 8 inches from front to rear. They range in color from green to brown and have dark bands on their legs and dark spots on their backs. They also have large eardrums on the sides of their heads.

Bullfrogs are native to the eastern U.S., but they have been introduced across the states for hunting (frog legs are considered a delicacy). They have also been introduced by frog-leg lovers to the Hawaiian Islands, Mexico, Cuba, Japan, and Italy.

Their booming *jug-o-rums* and *br-wums* can be heard around freshwater marshes, ponds, lakes, and streams on summer nights. Bullfrogs mate from late winter through spring. Masses of eggs are laid in water by females, and tadpoles soon emerge to eat algae and aquatic plants. It takes almost two years for a tadpole to develop into a bullfrog.

If you catch a bullfrog, it will pretend it's dead for a while. But don't worry, it's only "playing possum." After a few seconds, it will emit a *miaow* noise, then explode from your hands.

The bullfrog is one of 35 species of frogs and toads that live in the U.S. Two species, the Houston toad (*Bufo houstonensis*) and the Wyoming toad (*Bufo hemiophrys baxteri*), are endangered species.

On the wilderness trip, we kept hearing a baby crying. "It's nothing," the guide said. "We won't stop." The next morning Mom found mountain lion tracks, wider than her skis.

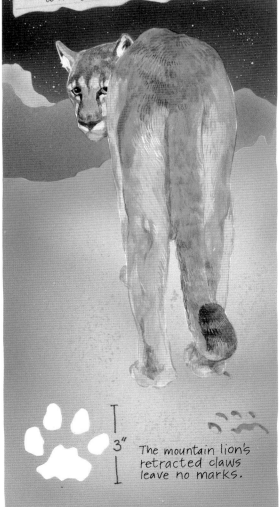

3"

The mountain lion's retracted claws leave no marks.

Armadillos

Armadillo is a Spanish word meaning "armored." Armadillos are unique because their bodies, tails, and heads are covered with a protective armorlike material that is made of small bony scales, which are all linked tightly together in bands. The gray bands of armor are attached to each other with leathery skin that lets the armadillo twist and move. They also have wirelike hairs all over their bodies.

Armadillos belong to an old family of animals found mostly in Central and South America, the Dasypodidae. Over 10,000 years ago, the ancestors of modern armadillos were the size of today's African rhinoceros. South America's giant armadillos are 3 feet long, and the tiny fairy armadillos are only 5 inches long. The nine-banded armadillo is about the size of a house cat. Its scientific name, *Dasypus novemcinctus*, means the "hairy-footed nine-banded" in Latin.

The nine-banded armadillo moved into Texas from Mexico about 100 years ago. It also lives in South America. It is now found throughout much of the southern U.S. and has been seen in Kansas and North Carolina.

The nine-banded armadillo can cross streams and small rivers by holding its breath and walking along the bottom. Or it can inflate its lungs and swim across.

Nine-bandeds live in burrows in woods and brushy areas, and farmers like them because they eat grubs, scorpions, fire ants, and other insects that damage crops.

They are also seen along highways at night, where many of the lumbering beasts are killed because they aren't good at getting out of the way. When startled by a predator, the nine-banded can jump 3 feet into the air. This usually frightens the predator so much that it runs away. If the predator persists, the nine-banded rolls up into a ball, so that only its armor is exposed.

Every spring, female armadillos give birth to exactly four young that are always the same sex. Scientists are not sure why. That is just the way nine-banded armadillos do things!

Opossums

The opossum (*Didelphis marsupialis*) is North America's only marsupial. Most marsupials live in Australia and Tasmania. Marsupials give birth to tiny young that crawl into their mother's pouch to nurse for several months and continue to develop before they emerge. Marsupials also have tails and hind toes that are prehensile so they can grab onto branches.

Baby opossums are born only 13 days after conception and are so small—1/15 ounce—that a dozen can fit into a teaspoon! After two months in the pouch, they are big enough to crawl out and hitch a ride on their mother's coarse gray fur as she goes out to eat at night.

Opossums live in most of the U.S., except for high mountain areas. They are easily recognized by their white faces and large ratlike tails. They survive by eating everything, from insects and fruit to dead animals. When attacked by predators, opossums just fall over and pretend to be dead. They "play possum."

Greenpatch Kid

A Bedroom Full of Frogs

Steven Cozza doesn't need to go camping to hear nighttime sounds and to sleep beneath the stars. He does that every night in his own room.

Steven and his family have so many animals that they jokingly call their house "The Cozza Zoo." The aviary in their backyard is home to quail, finches, doves, and canaries. They have chickens and rabbits running around their backyard. In the small pond Steven and his sister Anne helped build, goldfish swim around with bullfrog tadpoles. Inside the house is a large insect collection, Steven's dog Molly who lives with Anne's lovebird Frances, and thousands of silkworm eggs that rest in the family's refrigerator, waiting for spring.

But Steven's favorite animals are the frogs he raises in his bedroom terrarium. "I really like the frogs," says Steven, "because they make neat noises at night in my room." Steven has two treefrogs and four fire-belly frogs in his terrarium, along with a couple of lizards. The terrarium also has crickets that serve as frog and lizard food.

Steven's parents are always amazed when they walk into his room at night. "Every evening it sounds like Steven is in a swamp, because you hear the frogs and the crickets calling, and the lizards are scratching around," says Steven's dad. "And Steven has glow-in-the-dark stars all over his ceiling. So, it sounds, looks, and feels like you're outside. It's crazy, but Steven really enjoys it."

opossum using tail and rear thumbs to hang from branches

armadillo leaping to surprise predator.

opossum rear foot

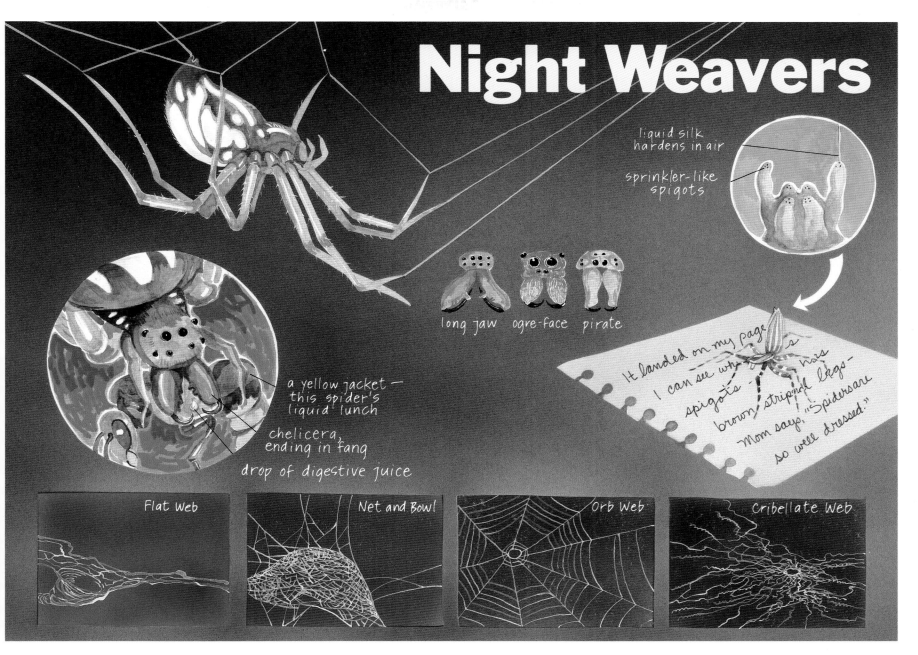

Night Weavers

liquid silk hardens in air

sprinkler-like spigots

long jaw   ogre-face   pirate

a yellow jacket — this spider's liquid lunch

chelicera ending in fang

drop of digestive juice

It landed on my page
I can see why...
spigots - has brown striped legs
Mom says, "Spiders are so well dressed."

Flat Web   Net and Bowl   Orb Web   Cribellate Web

Have you ever stepped outside at night and walked face first into a sticky cobweb? And what about that dust-covered web in the far corner of your bedroom ceiling that magically reappears after being torn down with a broom? Cobwebs are the work of night weavers: spiders.

Spiders are not insects. They lack the antennae, wings, and compound eyes of insects. Spiders are Arachnids, and they are related to scorpions, mites, and ticks. Most spiders are nocturnal and have three or four pairs of simple eyes arranged on the front of their head. Instead of insect mouthparts, spiders have fanglike structures called *chelicerae* for sucking juices from the insects they catch. They also have small arms next to their fangs for holding their victims.

Spiders are some of the oldest living animals on the earth, and there are an estimated 20,000 species worldwide. Fossilized spiders have been found that are 400 million years old!

Good Vibrations

Spiders have small bristles on their legs. The bristles are connected to nerves that can feel temperature, humidity, and air movement. Web-making spiders also use these bristles to feel web vibrations. They rest a sensitive front leg somewhere on their web and wait for the frantic movements of their captured prey.

All spiders are carnivorous, but they don't chew their food; they drink it. After capturing insects, spiders either restrain them with silk fibers or hold them with their front feet. They then inject a digestive fluid into the insects with their fanglike *chelicerae* and suck back liquefied tissue. Some larger spiders may look like they are chewing, but they are actually munching on the insects while turning them over and dripping digestive fluid on them. They then suck up the liquefied tissue from the mangled insects.

When courting, a male web-spinning spider approaches the female's web and gently taps the web to get the female's attention. He does so very carefully so he isn't mistaken for dinner. After mating, the female lays eggs and wraps them in silk. The eggs are then attached to the web, a nearby wall, or sometimes carried beneath the female until the young spiders emerge.

Silk Factory

Spider silk is a type of liquid protein called *fibroin*, and it is stretchier than artificial fibers (like nylon). The silk of orb spiders is the strongest natural fiber known.

A spider uses its hind legs to pull silk from its abdomen through tiny openings called *spigots*. Some spiders can pull out 2,300 feet of the microscopic silk at one time.

Cribellate spiders have spigots and a *cribellum*, a special spinning organ, that contains up to 40,000 additional spigots. The ultrafine silk produced by the cribellum is as little as 0.0007874 of an inch in diameter. It would take about 1,300 pieces of this fine silk, placed side by side, to equal 1 inch.

Because spider silk is a protein, many spiders, such as garden spiders (*Araneus*), eat their old webs before weaving new ones. That way the spider can recycle the protein in the old silk.

Web Wonders

Although most spiders can produce silk, not all make webs. Some spiders known as trap-door and wandering spiders chase their prey across the ground. Trap-door spiders line their burrows with silk and attach a lid with silk hinges. Because most of the 20,000 species of spiders build webs, there are many web shapes. Webs come in these four basic designs:

1. Flat matlike webs with tubular nest holes are spun by species such as funnel-web weavers and several common house spiders.

The spider waits in its tunnel, then runs out to grab the prey that falls on the web.

2. Disorganized netlike webs, often with a silk bowl placed on top, are built by comb-footed spiders and line-weaving spiders. These spiders live on the underside of the webs and run inside the bowl when they feel struggling prey. They quickly wrap the prey in silk and carry them away.

3. Round webs that are made of concentric circles with silk strands radiating from the center are the work of orb-web weavers. These are perhaps the most familiar webs because they are often attached to the sides of houses near lights, on fences, or strung between bushes. Orb spiders (there are probably several hundred species in the U.S. alone) can be spotted at night, either midweb waiting for insects, or on the web's edge.

4. Messy bands of fine silk are made by cribellate spiders outside and indoors. Most cribellates also make small tunnels in their webs where they wait in hiding for prey.

Webs are used and repaired all summer long, until winter rains and wind tear them apart. In winter, most spiders retreat to cracks in walls, sneak under boulders, or find underground tunnels. Many spiders die in the winter, but others can go without eating for long periods of time and live for several years, emerging each spring to spin again.

DJ calls it a Peanut Butter Spider. It's not in my field guide. Mrs. Jasper says there isn't much research done on spiders— except valuable or dangerous ones. Our notes may be the only ones there are! I asked, "If nobody studies them, how will they know which ones are important?"

Watching Night Weavers

Spiders are all around you, and most of them are active at night. If there are lights outside where you live, you can probably watch spiders at work without leaving your house. Leave on a porch light for a few nights. Insects will be drawn to the light. Spiders will follow the insects and set up shop.

Go on a spider safari with a flashlight. Look for trap-door and wandering spiders on the ground and web spiders in bushes or on fences. If you don't disturb their webs, most spiders will stay put and let you study them.

The best books for identifying the weavers in your backyard are *The Audubon Society Field Guide to North American Insects and Spiders* or *Eyewitness Junior Books, #4, Amazing Spiders*.

Fireflies

Photinus scintillans
long wings

male

stubby wings

female glowworm

larva,
also called glowworm

Glowworms feast on snails. First, they inject them with a liquefying fluid, then they suck them from their shells.

Microphotus angustus

male

female
pink glowworm

Some night creatures make their own light to attract each other. This yellow glow is called *bioluminescence*—the production of light by living organisms. The protein luciferin combines with oxygen inside these creatures to release energy in the form of yellow light (although sometimes it looks a little blue or green). This biochemical reaction is so efficient that no heat by-product is produced. Fireflies are the best-known producers of bioluminescence in the U.S.

Fireflies are actually flying beetles in the Lampyridae family (the "lamp" family), and there are over 100 U.S. species. They are common across the country except for parts of some western states. However, not all species produce light.

Firefly light is usually yellow, but in some species it can look light green or faint blue. In one western species called the pink glowworm (*Microphotus angustus*), only the wingless female glows a faint pink.

The males of glowing species, such as the pyralis firefly (*Photinus pyralis*), scintillating firefly (*Photinus scintillans*), Pennsylvania firefly (*Photuris pennsylvanica*), and two species with no common names, *Photinus marginellus* and *Photinus consanguineus*, begin flying just before sunset on summer evenings. They fly over fields and on the edges of woods. While flying, they flash a light in their abdomens using a specific pattern to attract females of the same species. Firefly flashing normally stops a few hours after sunset.

Pyralis males look like sparks coming up from the ground, because they fly in an undu-

lating pattern but always flash as they rise. *Photinus marginellus* and scintillating fireflies emit single quick flashes very similar in appearance as they fly in level patterns. *Photinus consanguineus* males produce sets of two short flashes, repeated over and over. Pennsylvania males either perch in treetops or fly above trees flashing up to five times in a row.

Female fireflies can't fly. They climb grass blades or branches, turn their abdomens upward and shake them back and forth in response to the males. Females are commonly called glowworms.

One disadvantage of this light is that it is also visible to predators or imitators. One predatory female firefly in the genus *Photuris* is able to mimic the light pattern of the female *Photinus* species. When *Photinus* males land to investigate, the mimicking *Photuris* female gobbles them up!

If you hold fireflies gently in your hand, or place them in a ventilated glass jar, you can watch at close range while they light up.

Rear segments flash as oxygen is pumped in.

On my little cousin's birthday I showed the kids how to catch fireflies without squeezing them, and let them go inside the paper lanterns. We had light through cake time.

Canned Bugs

Canned bugs? Many insects and spiders crawl about at night in search of prey or young vegetation to eat. To get a good look at some of these creatures without harming them, set a bug trap.

What you need:

coffee can or small bucket
piece of wood (big enough to cover the top of the container)
small rocks
shovel or spade

1. Choose a location where people do not walk.
2. Dig a hole just big enough for the container, so its top is level with the ground.
3. Place the container in the hole and place the rocks around the opening.
4. Place the wood on the rocks, so there is space between the top of the container and the bottom of the wood. This will let the bugs crawl in, but keep out larger animals and rain.
5. Leave your container overnight. Go out first thing in the morning and see what you caught.
6. After inspecting your catch, lift the can out, let the creatures go, then reset your trap.
You may want to maintain a bug trap in your yard for a year and keep a record of the species you collect in your nightwatch journal. Do some bugs get caught only at certain times of the year? Are some there all the time?

Make a Model Firefly

What you need:

old-style wooden clothespin
paper towels
transparent acetate, 3 by 6 inches
one aluminum drink can
2 feet of 14-gauge black solid wire
two 4-inch pieces of any thin wire
masking tape
acrylic paints
glow-in-the-dark acrylic paint
black indelible felt pen
white glue
Krazy Glue for wood
eye screw
metal file
tin snips and wire cutters
$\frac{1}{16}$-inch diameter drill
grown-up helper

1. Get a grown-up to help you with the knife work. Whittle off the end of one leg of the clothespin as shown. Trim the other into a rounded tail. With a sharp knife, carefully cut a slot in your firefly's back to hold its wings.
2. Ask your grown-up helper to drill two $\frac{1}{16}$-inch diameter holes through the body for the wire legs.
3. Insert lengths of the 14-gauge wire through the holes and the end of the clothespin slot to form the legs.
4. Bend into shape.
5. Fix each leg in place with Krazy Glue, then wrap them with masking tape next to the body.
6. Screw in eye screw behind the wing slot.
7. Ask your grown-up helper to cut open an aluminum can with the tin snips. Cut two outer wings, using pattern. Reverse the pattern for one wing to make a proper pair.
8. File the cut edges so they are less sharp.
9. Use the underwing pattern to trace and cut a pair of acetate wings.
10. Draw in veins with the black felt pen.
11. Saturate some strips of paper towel with white glue. Fold the towel to two thicknesses, about $\frac{3}{8}$ inch wide.
12. Wrap the end of the clothespin with successive layers of these bands to form the tail segments. Move from the tail end to midbody, then stop.
13. Using the hole at the front end of the clothespin, glue in two 4-inch thin wire antennae with Krazy Glue.
14. When the tail segments have dried, paint the body and upper wings dark brown or black. The second and third segments of the tail should be painted with the glow-in-the-dark paint. Since there are numerous species of fireflies with different markings, you will have a choice of how to decorate yours.
15. Glue the upper and underwings into the wing slot with Krazy Glue. Hang up your firefly with string tied through the eye screw and let it glow!

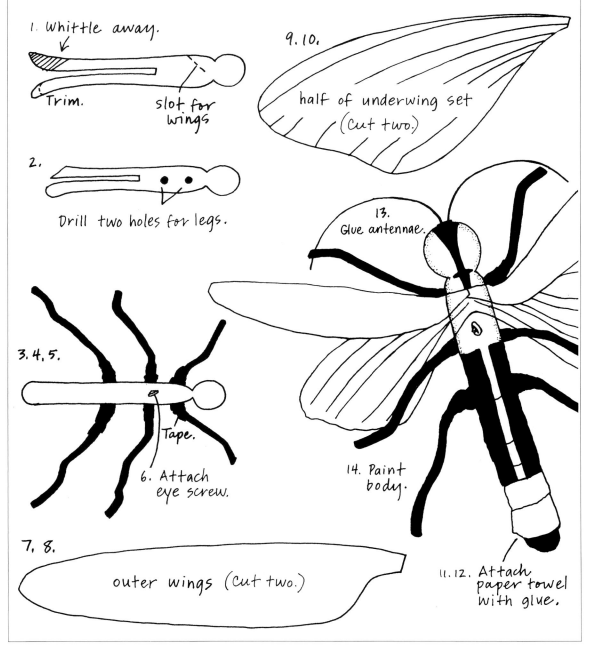

1. Whittle away. Trim. slot for wings

2. Drill two holes for legs.

9. 10. half of underwing set (cut two.)

3. 4. 5. Tape.

6. Attach eye screw.

13. Glue antennae.

14. Paint body.

7. 8. outer wings (cut two.)

11. 12. Attach paper towel with glue.

Houseguests

The small webs throughout your rooms are the work of common house spiders. Small, thin bowllike webs attached to the corners and windows are probably the work of the variously colored ¼-inch *Theridium tepidariorum*. Another species, *Steatoda borealis*, is also about ¼ inch long but has an orange-brown body and spins "snares" in similar locations.

Thick, flat webs with cavelike entrances are made by yellow-and-gray *Tegenaria domestica*. In cellars and underneath stairs, *Pholcus phalangioides* (sometimes called "daddy longlegs") attach thin webs using their 2-inch legs. All of these houseguests are harmless.

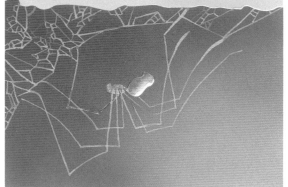

There are nervous daddy longlegs in our camping cooler in the creek. I reach in, and they thump their bodies on the lid: BOOM BOOM BOOM

The American cockroach (*Periplaneta americana*) is one of the earth's oldest creatures, and it is able to eat just about anything. There are nearly 60 cockroach species in the U.S. and more than 3,500 worldwide! Many U.S. species are introduced, and most live in the southern states. The American cockroach is 1½ inches long, brown, and disliked by most humans. When the kitchen lights flick on at night, cockroaches scramble back to their hiding places behind cabinets and under appliances.

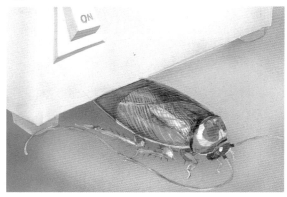

There are 24 species of mice in the U.S., but the common house mouse (*Mus musculus*) is the only one that might be living in your home. It can begin reproducing when only six weeks old and has three or four litters yearly with up to 11 babies in each litter. Only 6 inches long from head to tail, the house mouse can slip through tiny cracks in walls and floors. It is omnivorous, and it will even chase down cockroaches for a meal.

Dogs, aquarium fish, parakeets, and most other pets rest at night. But if you have a cat you might hear it chasing the mouse that is chasing the cockroach.

Greenpatch Kid

His Favorite Is the Cockroach

Ten years ago, when Brian Pacula was only three years old, he started watching and collecting insects. Over the years, his collection has grown to more than 200 species. He really likes large moths, such as lunas, polyphemus, and ceanothus, but his favorite insect is the cockroach.

Although Brian's mom, Pam, thinks his interest in insects is great, his brothers don't share Brian's enthusiasm. "They went berserk the first time Brian brought cockroaches into the house," says Pam. "They get grossed out with all of the insects that end up on our kitchen table."

"I have no idea why I like cockroaches," states Brian. "I mean, they're so easy to hate. But here I am, one of the six or seven people in the world, not counting pesticide company executives, who like roaches. Most people spend money trying to get rid of cockroaches, and I actually go out of my way to get them. I actually bought some! Yep." Brian believes cockroaches are some of the toughest and smartest animals alive. They have been on the earth a long time, he will tell you. They can develop immunity against poison, and they can live without eating for weeks. "I don't know any humans that can do that," says Brian.

Brian likes to look for insects at night. "I wait until the porch light has been on awhile, then I go outside and see what's there. It's really great. Sometimes I've found sphinx moths that way."

Sea of Tranquility was the site of the moon landing 7/20/69.

Smooth and dark, moon "seas" are solid lava under a thin coat of dust.

Beetle in the Moon

Rabbit in the Moon

Reading Lady in the Moon

Tide pool life soaks and dries in sync with the circling moon.

Moon Watch

You and your friends are playing outside on a warm summer night. Overhead, a brilliant full moon lights your way. As you race around, your legs blur with continuous motion in the moonlight. You dash in and out of the moon shadows, squealing with laughter, bursting with coyote howls, and electrified with excitement. It seems as though you will never tire, and your night of moon play will never end.

You and your friends are not alone. Many creatures celebrate under the light of the full moon. Cottontail rabbits congregate for full moon "dances." They bolt toward each other, leap into the air, boxing with all four legs, land, touch noses, then sprint toward another dancing partner. Wolves, coyotes, and domestic dogs howl louder and longer, it seems. Cats fight and scream, deer dance about, and the bushes and woods rustle with activity all night.

Not too long ago, people thought that during full moons humans could become werewolves, that witches were more active, and that spirits walked about. The word *lunatic*, which means a crazy person, is Latin for "related to the moon." The words *moonstruck* and *moony* are used to describe a person who is acting overly sentimental or strange.

Many people believe in the power of the moon during all of its phases. It was once common for people to consult the phases of the moon to decide the best time to have babies, schedule elections, travel, and more. Talk to serious gardeners, and they will tell you to plant seeds and seedlings during a full moon so the plants will grow faster and stronger.

This all seems possible, doesn't it? After all, the moon (with some help from the sun) causes Earth's ocean tides. As it orbits Earth, the moon's gravitational pull creates a bulge on the ocean's surface, directly beneath it. As Earth turns, this bulge moves across the oceans, and tides rise and fall in its path.

Moon Matters

There are different ideas about how the moon was formed. The fission theory claims that the moon was once part of Earth and was ripped away when Earth was softer and rotated faster. The collision theory states that Earth was hit by a large asteroid and a chunk of Earth came off to form the moon. The capture theory maintains that the moon was formed in space but came close to Earth and was "captured" by Earth's gravitational pull. The ring theory states that Earth once had a ring-shaped band of material surrounding it that collapsed to form the moon.

The most favored theory is the binary theory. It states that Earth and the moon were formed separately, but close together, from cosmic dust about 5 billion years ago.

The moon orbits Earth at an average distance of 239,000 miles, and it is 2,160 miles across (Earth's diameter is almost 8,000 miles). The moon takes 27.3 days to orbit the globe, the exact amount of time the moon needs to rotate once on its axis. Because of this fact, you are *always* looking at the same side of the moon.

You probably grew up hearing about "The Man in the Moon," the image created by the moon's mountains and dark plains on the side we always see. But in other parts of the world people look at the same moon and see a woman, a rabbit, a coyote, a crab, a bear, or other animals. Look at the full moon with a telescope or binoculars. What do *you* see?

Moon Phases

Just like the sun and the stars, the moon rises in the east and sets in the west as a result of Earth's rotation from west to east. But the moon is actually circling around Earth from west to east. Because the moon is moving in the same direction as Earth, it *looks like* it moves across the night sky more slowly than the sun and stars. In fact, the time the moon rises and sets is about 50 minutes later each day.

New Moon. At new moon, the real new moon is located between Earth and the sun and rises and sets almost exactly with the sun. Because the moon has no light of its own (it reflects sunshine like the planets), you *don't see* real new moons because the sunlight is hitting the side of the moon that faces away from Earth.

Waxing Crescent. Because the moon rises about 50 minutes later every day, a few days after the real new moon you can see a thin crescent at sunset. It is called a waxing crescent. This thin crescent is what you know as the new moon. Waxing means it's getting bigger. It's a crescent because it is reflecting sunshine from its side, the right side. Look for the waxing crescent moon low in the western sky. It sets after the sun.

First Quarter. About a week after the new moon, the moon is in a phase called first quarter. Really, though, it appears as a half circle, lit up on its right side and rising at about noon. It stays in the sky for half the night.

Waxing Gibbous. Gibbous means hump. The waxing gibbous moon has a small hump projecting to the left. Now the moon is rising in the afternoon, and it stays in the sky almost all night.

Full Moon. Now the moon is on the opposite side of Earth from the sun and rises at about sunset and sets about sunrise.

Waning Gibbous. The full moon begins to wane, which means disappear. Darkness creeps in from the right side of the moon, making the hump on that side. The left side stays fully illuminated.

Last Quarter. The moon wanes even more until it reduces to another half disk, this time reflecting on its left side. It has been about three weeks now since the new moon. The waning half moon is now rising about six hours before the sun and setting at noon, so you can only see it in the morning.

Waning Crescent. The moon is a small crescent again, but it is lit up on its left side. It rises just before sunrise and sets in the afternoon. In a few days the new moon rises, and the cycle starts all over.

Full Moon Names

Because people once closely timed their activities with the phases of the moon, every full moon was given at least one name, and often two or three.

The harvest moon is the full moon that rises closest to the autumnal equinox (when the day has 12 hours of sun and 12 hours of darkness). Some years the harvest moon rises in September, other years in October. Most calendars include the date for each year's autumnal equinox.

When any month has two full moons, the second one is *always* called the blue moon. Blue moons don't happen very often, which is why we have the saying "Once in a blue moon."

January Old Moon, Moon after Yule
February Snow Moon, Hunger Moon, Wolf Moon
March Sap Moon, Cow Moon, Lenten Moon
April Grass Moon, Egg Moon
May Planting Moon, Milk Moon
June Rose Moon, Flower Moon, Strawberry Moon
July Thunder Moon, Hay Moon
August Green Corn Moon, Grain Moon
September Fruit Moon (Harvest Moon)
October Hunter's Moon (Harvest Moon)
November Frosty Moon, Beaver Moon
December Long Night Moon, Moon before Yule

Birds of the August Moon

There are too many bird species that migrate at night to list them all. Birds use a variety of signals to navigate nocturnally: Earth's magnetic field, the stars, the moon, the sun, and even smells.

But why fly at night? One good reason is to avoid daytime predatory birds. Also, weather conditions, especially winds, might be more favorable at night. Some night-migrating birds fly close to the ground, but geese have been recorded at 21,000 feet by airline pilots!

In August, September, or October, when the full moon is hanging in the sky, you can see the distant silhouettes of night-migrating birds as they fly across the face of the moon. But you need patience, a pair of binoculars, and a comfortable chair.

Find out when the full moon rises during those three months (most calendars will tell you). Get your telescope or binoculars and your chair, and when the full moon is up, go outside and get ready. It is best if you can steady your elbows on a chair's arms or on a railing. Focus on the moon and wait for the silhouettes of migrating birds as they fly between you and the moon. Because they are so far away, you won't be able to identify the exact species of birds you see.

Remember, you are looking at a small section of a very large sky, but on a good night you will see lots of birds, if you're willing to wait awhile (it's worth it!). How many birds fly across your moon?

As the moon rose, we saw swans flying high. The little birds stay lower to the ground.

Eclipses

Scientists believe prehistoric people were frightened during lunar (moon) eclipses because they thought the moon was disappearing forever. In some parts of the world today, people run outside screaming and banging pots during eclipses, trying to scare away the "evil spirits" who are taking away their moon.

In a solar eclipse the moon comes directly between Earth and the sun and blocks the sunlight. The shadow the moon casts on Earth makes it dark during the day. In a lunar eclipse Earth is between the sun and the moon. Earth's shadow gradually moves across the moon and obscures its light.

The moon's orbit around Earth is on a slightly different plane than Earth's orbit around the sun. If it was in the same plane as Earth's, then we would have a solar eclipse every new moon (moon blocking sun), and a total lunar eclipse every full moon (Earth blocking sun).

When the new moon's orbit intersects with Earth's every now and again, we get a solar eclipse. When the full moon's orbit intersects with Earth's, we get a lunar eclipse.

Lunar Eclipses 1994 to 2000

YEAR AND DATE	TIME OF MID-ECLIPSE*	TYPE AND LENGTH OF ECLIPSE (MINS.)**
1994, May 25	3:32	Partial
1995, April 15	12:19	Partial
1996, April 4	0:11	Total (86)
1996, Sept. 27	2:55	Total (70)
1997, March 24	4:41	Partial
1997, Sept. 16	18:47	Total (62)
1999, July 28	11:34	Partial
2000, Jan. 21	4:45	Total (76)
2000, July 16	13:57	Total (106)

*Times are Greenwich Mean Time, 24-hour standard. Subtract 5 hours for Eastern Standard Time, 6 hours for Central Standard Time, 7 hours for Mountain Standard Time, and 8 hours for Pacific Standard Time. If the eclipses occur between sunset and sunrise, then you are apt to see the eclipse.
**No length of time is given for partial eclipses.

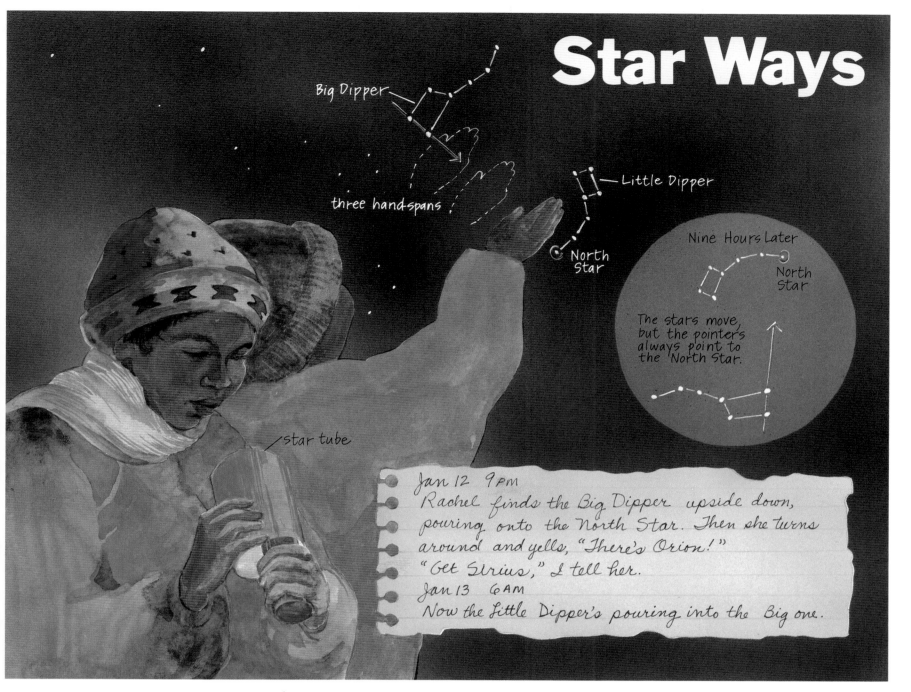

Star Ways

Big Dipper

three handspans

Little Dipper

North Star

Nine Hours Later

North Star

The stars move, but the pointers always point to the North Star.

star tube

Jan 12 9 PM
Rachel finds the Big Dipper upside down, pouring onto the North Star. Then she turns around and yells, "There's Orion!"
"Get Sirius," I tell her.
Jan 13 6 AM
Now the Little Dipper's pouring into the Big one.

Satellite Patrol

There are almost 2,100 active satellites orbiting Earth at this very moment (some are below your feet right now). About 5,000 pieces of space garbage (dead satellites, old booster rockets, nuts, and bolts) are also orbiting up there. Another 2,300 satellites have either fallen into Earth's atmosphere and disintegrated or been lost in space, and around 13,000 pieces of space garbage have left our orbit, burned up, or fallen to the earth. There is so much stuff up there that companies have asked the U.S. government if they can rent a space shuttle to collect the debris, fix it up, and sell it!

The government keeps track of everything in the sky so space shuttles don't run into any of it. You and I don't know how powerful our radars and satellites are (it's a government secret), but an astronaut's glove was once tracked from Earth as an experiment.

Many satellites (active and dead) are visible every night as they zip quietly above your head in the shadow of our planet. A satellite reflects the sun's rays and looks like a *moving* solid dot of light.

Most satellites fly between 150 and 300 miles above Earth. They are so close to Earth (in space dimensions) that they are quickly obscured by Earth's shadow after sunset. That's why it is best to look for them just after dusk or just before dawn.

People have traveled with the help of the stars for centuries. Before highways, maps, electricity, flashlights, and compasses, people memorized star songs and star stories that helped them find their way at night. Polynesian sailors could navigate for days between distant islands using their knowledge of how the stars were arranged. Even today, airplane pilots have to know the stars in case their sophisticated guidance equipment fails during a night flight.

Before you jump outside into the dark to learn how things work in the night sky, you need to orient yourself. Find out what is where. Can you step outside right now, without a compass, and point directly north?

Where on Earth Am I?

There is an easy way you can find which way is north without a compass. First, you have to locate the Big Dipper—one of the best-known constellations in our night sky. With the help of this drawing and your star tube (see page 34), you'll soon recognize the Big Dipper (also known as Ursa Major, the Great Bear).

Got it? Now, locate the two stars on the Big Dipper's bowl farthest away from the handle. These are called the pointers because they *point* to the North Star. Draw an imaginary line that connects the pointers and extend it beyond the opening of the bowl until you reach a solitary bright star. If you use the back of your hand held out in front of you as a measuring stick, the North Star is about three or four hand-spans away. You are now looking north!

Face the North Star. To your right is east, to your left is west, and south is behind you. Now, no matter where you go in the U.S., you'll always be able to get your bearings by looking at the night sky (unless it's completely cloudy!).

Because it aligns with Earth's axis above the North Pole, the North Star is also called the Pole Star. As Earth revolves, its axis remains still. Because of this, the North Star never appears to move. All other stars and constellations revolve around the North Star, counterclockwise.

Make a Star Tube

Here is how you can find the Big Dipper and other constellations in the night sky.

What you need:
empty oatmeal container (the tubelike kind)
large nail
flashlight

The oatmeal container is your star tube. Turn the tube upside down and draw the Big Dipper on the bottom, using dots for the stars. (Use the drawing below as a guide.) Punch holes with the nail where you drew the dots. Write the name of the constellation on the box.

Take your star tube and your flashlight outside at night and hold the flashlight inside the tube. The holes you punched in the bottom will look like the stars in the Big Dipper. Look at the star pattern carefully. Now turn off your flashlight and search the sky until you find the real constellation.

Collect more oatmeal containers so you can make star tubes for the Little Dipper, Cassiopeia, the Dragon, and any other constellations you want.

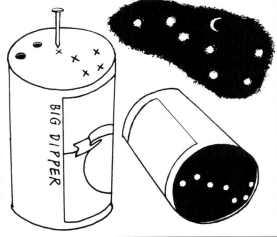

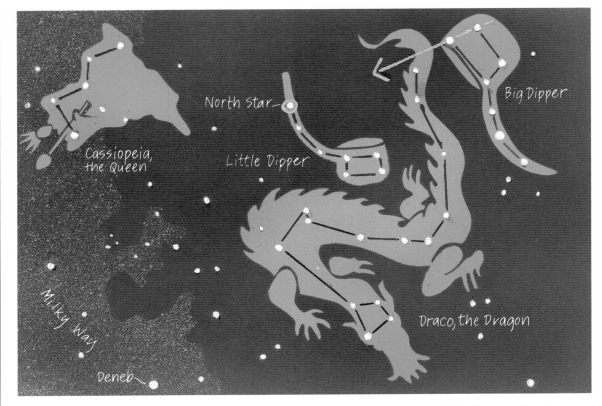

Circumpolar Constellations

Now that you know how to find the Big Dipper, the North Star, and your compass directions, how about those other stars revolving around the North Star? Together with the Big Dipper, they make up the circumpolar constellations and are constant nighttime companions. Here are the three brightest circumpolar constellations:

Little Dipper (Ursa Minor). The Little Dipper looks like a smaller and dimmer version of the Big Dipper, except the Little Dipper's handle curves up, not down. The North Star is the tip of the Little Dipper's handle. If you live in a city, you may not be able to see the entire Little Dipper.

Draco, the Dragon. The Dragon is a large constellation, but not extremely bright. The Dragon's long tail winds between the bowls of the two dippers, and its head is almost a quadrangle, about half the size of the Big Dipper's bowl.

Cassiopeia, the Queen. Appearing as a neat-shaped W in the sky, Cassiopeia not only revolves around the North Star, but it's in the Milky Way. So, when you find Cassiopeia, you're also looking at the Milky Way. The North Star is between Cassiopeia and the Big Dipper. Cassiopeia is almost directly across from the Big Dipper's pointers. And just like the Big Dipper, Cassiopeia is about three or four hand-spans away from the North Star.

The galactic pie as if cut in half: gas, dust, and millions of stars.

galactic core of older red stars

cross section of the galaxy: the Milky Way

spiral arms of the galaxy: hot, younger blue stars

position of our sun

A Slice of Galactic Pie

If you live in a city, the Milky Way may be something you only read about in books. But it's really up there: a vast stream of stars and cosmic dust stretching across our galaxy. The dark patches in the Milky Way aren't holes, but bands of the cosmic dust that obscure the stars.

This starry necklace across the night sky is really a slice of our galactic pie—a sideways glance across our galaxy. Every star you see in the sky is part of our galaxy, a spiralling mass that is shaped like a pancake and pinwheel combined, consisting of a hundred billion stars.

The sun (the star closest to us) and its nine planets are located more than halfway out toward the edge of the galaxy and are one tiny speck in this enormous galactic pie. Imagine our galaxy as a large pancake filled with stars. When you look up at night and see that irregular milky white ribbon across the sky, you are really looking sideways across that pancake of stars. You are looking across the galaxy.

Because of the way Earth orbits the sun, you are looking more toward the center of the galaxy in summer than in winter. Since there are more stars toward the center, the Milky Way is brighter in summer than winter. If you

can get away from bright city lights, the Milky Way is visible year-round. On a clear, moonless night, away from lights, this starry stream can be so bright you won't mistake it for anything else. But if you aren't sure where it is, look for the constellation Cassiopeia (see above) and the stars Altair and Deneb (see page 35). Cassiopeia, Altair, and Deneb are *in* the Milky Way, so when you find them, draw an imaginary line across the sky connecting them, and you will slowly be able to see the Milky Way.

Standout Stars

Getting to know a few of the brightest stars in the night sky will help you orient yourself even better during your nocturnal ventures. Instead of just being stars, they can become signposts, timekeepers, and indicators of seasonal change.

Although it may seem like you can spot millions of stars some nights, your eyes can only see about 2,000 stars on the darkest and clearest evening. There are 88 constellations in the entire sky. About 60 can be seen from the U.S. throughout the year, but at any given time of night you can only view about a dozen. There are approximately 30 very bright stars. Here are seven:

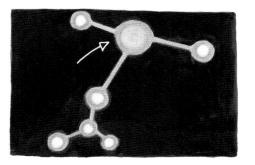

Sirius. The brightest in the entire sky, Sirius means "scorcher" in Greek. Sirius is part of the Big Dog constellation, which you can see on the southern horizon most of the year. Because it is low on the horizon, it takes a very clear night to see the other stars in the constellation besides Sirius. On some star maps the Big Dog is labeled with its Latin name, Canis Major. Sirius and the Big Dog can be found in the sky by extending the line made by Orion's belt southward about three hand-spans.

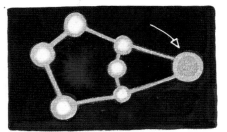

Arcturus. The fourth brightest star is a beautiful orange color—25 times bigger than our sun and 100 times as bright (if viewed from the same distance). To find Arcturus (part of the Herdsman [Bootes] constellation) follow the arc of the Big Dipper's handle away from the bowl, until you spy a very bright star. That's Arcturus.

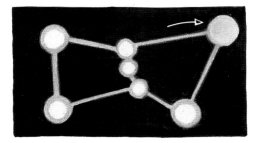

Rigel. The seventh brightest star is located in the constellation Orion, below Orion's well-known belt (three stars in a row). Rigel is Orion's foot. This bluish white star is enormous—33 times the diameter of our sun and 46,000 times brighter. It is so far away that the light you see left Rigel over 900 years ago.

Your Bedroom Solar System

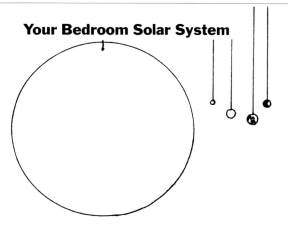

By making a model of the solar system on your ceiling or wall, you'll always remember how the planets are arranged. The key to making the model is to use a variation of the Astronomical Unit (AU).

One AU is the average distance between Earth and the sun, about 92,956,600 miles. Even if you live in a barn, a real-scale model won't fit. Instead, use 2 inches as your AU. That means the planets would be the following distances from the sun:

Mercury	¾ inch
Venus	1½ inches
Earth	2 inches (AU)
Mars	3 inches
Jupiter	10½ inches
Saturn	19 inches
Uranus	38 inches
Neptune	60 inches
Pluto	78 inches

A real-scale model is also impossible because the sun's diameter is 870,000 miles, and the diameter of Pluto, the smallest planet, is only 1,400 miles. So, following this order, from the biggest to the smallest—Sun, Jupiter, Saturn, Uranus, Neptune, Earth, Venus, Mars, Mercury, Pluto—cut out the sun and the planets from cardboard or heavy paper. Make the sun about a foot across and scale down from there. Color your sun and planets if you like, paint them with glow-in-the-dark paint, or write their names on them.

Mark off the above distances on your ceiling or wall, and place pushpins at each mark. Take pieces of thread and attach them with glue or tape to your cutout sun and planets, then tie them to the pushpins.

Antares. The reddish Antares means "the rival of Mars" in Greek. It is located in the Scorpion (Scorpio) constellation (just below its claws), and is number 16 in brightness. Mars, the "Red Planet," travels close to Antares and can be confused with this Mars look-alike. The Scorpion skirts our southern horizon during the summer months, then dips below the horizon in winter.

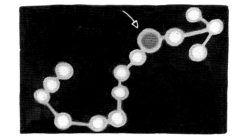

Vega. White Vega, part of the constellation Lyra, is the fifth brightest star in the night sky and 50 times brighter than our sun. But Vega is 26 light-years away (the distance light travels in a year), and the sun is only 8½ light-minutes away. Our solar system is moving toward Vega at 12 miles per second. At that rate, we should bump into Vega in about 500,000 years. The head of the Dragon constellation (one of our circumpolar constellations) points toward Vega.

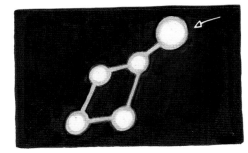

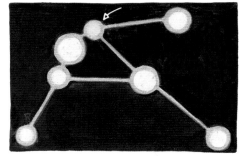

Altair. The eye of the Eagle constellation, this yellowish white star is number 12 in brightness. The Eagle is a beautiful little constellation "flying" down the Milky Way. When you find Altair (go from the Dragon's head to Vega and then beyond to Altair), you have found the Milky Way. On some star maps the Eagle is labeled by its Latin name, Aquila.

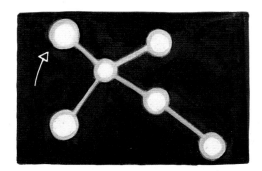

Deneb. This is the brightest star in the Swan constellation (Cygnus in Latin). Deneb is 1,600 light-years away and about 50,000 times brighter than the sun. Like Altair, when you find Deneb, you are also looking at the Milky Way.

The Summer Triangle. The stars Vega, Altair, and Deneb form a large triangle in the summer sky familiar to all navigators. Can you find it?

Celestial Treasure Hunt

Joining the standout stars in the night sky are a big family of celestial treasures: auroras, binary stars, galaxies, gas clouds, nebulas, planets, star clusters, and variable stars. Take a friend or two, go outside with your telescope or binoculars, and have a celestial treasure hunt. Here are three prime treasures to start you on your way.

When you first look at the night sky with a telescope or binoculars, your field of vision will be packed with stars. Don't be overwhelmed. It will take a few times of looking through your lens, then using your bare eye, to find what you're looking for. And, while you're looking, you'll see some amazing stuff!

Andromeda nebula

Andromeda Nebula

The Andromeda nebula is found in the Andromeda constellation. To find the constellation look south of the W formed by the constellation Cassiopeia. Close to the bent knee of Andromeda you'll find a small hazy spot (easier to see on a moonless night).

That's the Andromeda nebula. *Nebula* means "misty cloud," which is what this distant galaxy looks like to the human eye. This galaxy is very similar to ours. It might look like a cosmic smudge in the night sky, but it is composed of billions of stars and is some 2.7 million light-years away.

The Andromeda nebula is the most distant object the human eye can see without a telescope. Once you've found it you'll be able to see it on moonless nights without your telescope or binoculars.

Pleiades

The cluster of stars known as the Pleiades makes up the tip of a horn in Taurus, the Bull constellation. To find the Pleiades, look in the sky between Cassiopeia, Andromeda, and Orion. (Go to Orion's belt, then go five to six hand-spans to the northwest.) When you first see it, this tight group of stars will look a bit

Pleiades

blue dust clouds

Greenpatch Kid

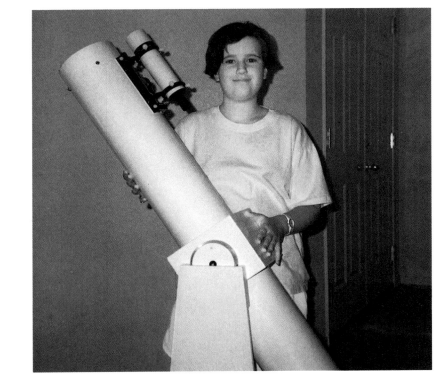

She Built Her Own Telescope

To most people, sewer pipes, plywood, and plastic sink drains don't sound like parts for a telescope, but they do to Jamie Ghiringhelli and her dad, Jim. That's because Jamie and her dad built a telescope using these parts and a few others when Jamie was ten years old. Since then Jamie has joined her local Junior Astronomical Club and spends many nights stargazing. Jamie and Jim have started building a second telescope with ten of Jamie's school classmates, and they are grinding their own telescope lens. "Grinding the lens is fairly technical stuff," says Jim. "But we are having a great time, learning a bunch, and not spending a lot of money."

"I really like looking at the Andromeda galaxy and the Orion nebula," says Jamie. "They're my favorites." But Jamie believes stargazing takes some practice, and that not all celestial bodies are easy to find. "Some nebulas are hard to find," says Jamie. "Like, the Beehive nebula. I looked for a long time, but I finally found it." Although Jamie spends many hours using her telescope to observe stars and planets, she has her sights on a bigger goal. "I want to be one of the first people to step onto another planet. I've wanted to be an astronaut since I was little. To do that you have to study a lot of math and know a lot about stars, but it will be fun."

like a nebula, or a miniature (and messy) Big Dipper. If you look carefully with your bare eye, however, you can distinguish six individual stars. With a telescope or binoculars, you will see more than six stars.

Although they appear close to one another from your perspective, the stars that form the Pleiades are actually light-years apart.

Orion's Gas

Orion is the dominant constellation of your southern night sky. (Remember the star Rigel is one of Orion's feet.) Take a close look at the three stars that make up Orion's belt. They are each about one of your fingers apart from each other. Together these three stars form one of the straightest lines in the night sky.

Below Orion's belt are another three (fainter) stars in a straight line called Orion's

sword. The middle star of the sword is actually a giant gas cloud. It is called the Great Orion nebula, a luminous gas cloud so enormous that 10,000 stars the size of our sun could be formed from its mass.

New stars are still being formed out of Orion's gas.

Your Own Telescope

Would you like to see Saturn's rings and Jupiter's moons? Or the moon's enormous craters? Would you like to scan the Milky Way for distant galaxies? Most telescopes are elaborate and expensive pieces of equipment. But here is a design for one you can build yourself out of materials that you have around the house, except for the lenses. Those you need to buy (see box). If you take the time to make this instrument, you will see things you can't see otherwise, and everything you see will be special because you made the telescope yourself.

This is a simple astronomical telescope, so it produces inverted images. This means that what you see will appear upside down and backward through the telescope lenses. But don't worry. When viewing most celestial objects in the night sky, it doesn't matter if their image is inverted. However, it does take a little getting used to, especially since you'll be tempted to move the telescope in the opposite direction than you think you are moving it when you aim it at something.

What you need:
two standard file folders (30 cm × 45 cm)
tape (almost any kind will do)
objective lens (plastic, about 50 mm
    diameter, between 500 and 700 mm focal
    length)
eyepiece lens (plastic, 50 mm or less in
    diameter, between 50 and 90 mm focal
    length)
metric ruler (all measurements are in
    centimeters, cm, or millimeters, mm)
scissors
paper glue
dime and quarter
pencil
copy machine

First Some Notes

Your telescope has seven pieces (Figure 1). It has two main sections. The outer sliding tube holds the objective lens, and the inner sliding tube holds the eyepiece lens.

Telescope Pieces

1. Measuring ring (cut from folder:
    1 cm × 18 cm)
2. Objective lens
3. Outer sliding tube (cut from folder:
    22 cm × 44 cm)
4. Inner sliding tube (cut from folder:
    30 cm × 44 cm)
5. Eyepiece lens
6. Eyepiece holder (cut from folder:
    8 cm × 20 cm)
7. Eye-centering disk (cut from folder:
    traced from objective lens)

The first time you assemble the telescope, ask a grown-up to assist you. Also, use tape, not glue. If the tape unsticks after a while, use a tiny spot of glue on the file folder stock before retaping, except where noted. When rolling tubes from folders, it's best to roll the tube into a smaller diameter than needed, then let the tube spring back

out to the needed size. You can lay out the pieces on standard file folders as shown in Figure 2. Mark with ruler and pencil, and cut out the pieces with scissors. Label the pieces as you go so you don't forget which is which.

Lenses

Lenses vary slightly in diameter and focal length (power). That's okay. As long as you have one objective lens and one eyepiece lens that fall within the dimensions listed above, they'll work fine. Both of these lenses are called *double convex lenses* in stores and in scientific catalogs. This name is important to remember when buying lenses. Here are two ways you can buy the lenses needed for this activity.

1. Call or write the Discovery Corner and ask about the lens packet they sell for file folder telescopes. The packet (both lenses) should cost around $3.00. *The Discovery Corner, Lawrence Hall of Science, University of California, Berkeley, CA 94720. Phone 510-642-1016.*

2. Call or write Edmund Scientific and ask for one of their free Optics, Science, and Education Catalogs. When you receive it, look under double convex lenses or plano lenses, educational grade or experimental grade. Then you can use their form to either mail your order, or phone it in. The cost of both lenses should total about $9.00. *Edmund Scientific, 101 E. Gloucester Pike, Barrington, NJ 08007-1380.* Phone 609-573-6250 or 609-547-3488.

Note: It is important to buy one of these lenses to use as your objective lens. But if you find an inexpensive, hand-held lens in a science or hobby store that fits the dimensions needed for the eyepiece lens, buy it and use it.

Assembly

1. Wrap the measuring ring piece (#1) around the objective lens (#2) to form a ring that the objective lens just barely fits into. Once the ring is straight and just the right size, tape it as shown in Figure 3. Remove the lens.

2. Roll the outer sliding tube piece (#3) into a tube about 44 cm long and slide it into the measuring ring until the ring is at its center. Let the tube spring open to the size of the measuring ring. Line up the edges and corners of the tube as straight as possible so the tube is a constant diameter all the way down its length. Put a piece of tape on the seam of the tube just next to the measuring ring to keep the tube from springing open. Slide the measuring ring over one end of the tube and tape that end as shown in Figure 4. Slide the measuring ring to the other end of the tube and tape that end as well. Then tape down the entire length of the tube's seam.

3. Roll the folder piece for the inner sliding tube (#4) into a tube about 44 cm long. Insert it into the outer sliding tube, leaving a few centimeters extending out one end. Make sure the edges of the inner sliding tube are straight, then tape its exposed corner (Figure 5). Slide the inner sliding tube farther into the outer tube, until the other end of the inner tube extends a few centimeters beyond that of the outer tube. Tape that corner. Then put tape along the entire length of the inner tube by sliding it either way as needed to expose more of its seam for taping.

4. Trace the outline of the objective lens onto a piece of scrap folder so it can be made into the eye-centering disk (#7) later. Also, trace the outline of the objective lens onto the center of the pattern for the eyepiece holder (#6) as shown in Figure 6. The eyepiece holder pattern will be cut out of folder stock in Step 6. To do so, make a photocopy of the eyepiece holder pattern and use the cutout pattern from the photocopy to glue onto the file folder stock.

5. Tape the objective lens onto one end of the outer sliding tube. Start by putting two small pieces of tape at opposite edges of the lens, covering as little of the lens as possible. After attaching the lens to the tube with those small pieces of tape, you can put more small pieces of tape around the lens to secure it to the tube as shown in Figure 7.

6. Glue the pattern for the eyepiece holder onto the appropriate folder piece (#6). After it has dried, put a quarter (25¢) at the center of the pattern and trace the outline of the quarter with a pencil. Cut out the circle that you just traced. Then, cut out the rest of the eyepiece holder along the dashed lines down to where you marked the outline of the objective lens (in Step 4) and along the outline of the objective lens, but not through the shaded area of the long tabs. Then, make a number of small cuts (about 4 mm long) inward from the outline of the objective lens to make short tabs, each about a centimeter wide (Figure 6).

7. Bend up the short tabs and the long tabs as shown in Figure 8. Tape the eyepiece lens over the center hole, using small pieces of tape and covering as little of the lens as possible.

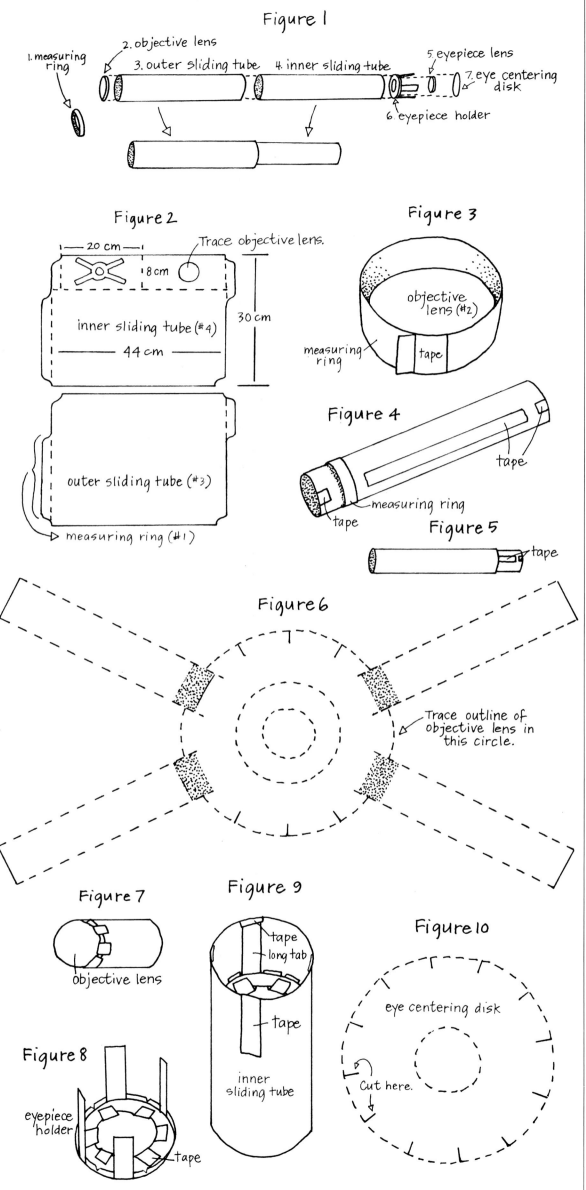

Figure 1

1. measuring ring
2. objective lens
3. outer sliding tube
4. inner sliding tube
5. eyepiece lens
6. eyepiece holder
7. eye centering disk

Figure 2

20 cm
8 cm
Trace objective lens.
inner sliding tube (#4)
44 cm
30 cm
outer sliding tube (#3)
measuring ring (#1)

Figure 3

objective lens (#2)
measuring ring
tape

Figure 4

tape
measuring ring
tape

Figure 5

tape

Figure 6

Trace outline of objective lens in this circle.

Figure 7

objective lens

Figure 8

eyepiece holder
tape

Figure 9

tape
long tab
tape
inner sliding tube

Figure 10

eye centering disk
Cut here.

8. Slide the eyepiece lens and eyepiece holder assembly down into the inner sliding tube at the end opposite from the objective lens, lens first. The long tabs should all extend down the tube the same distance so the eyepiece lens is held straight in the tube. The end of each long tab can be taped flush with the end of the inner sliding tube (Figure 9). Do not glue.

9. The telescope is fairly sensitive to the position of your eye in front of the lens. Your eye needs to be in line with the center of the eyepiece lens for best results. That's why you need an eye-centering disk (Figure 10) over the end of the inner sliding tube.

Use the piece of folder on which you marked the first outline of the objective lens (Step 4). Use a dime to mark a small circle within the circle, centering it as carefully as you can.

Cut out the dime-sized circle. Then cut out the larger disk. Make tabs as shown, then tape the disk onto the end of the inner sliding tube. Do not glue.

Congratulations! Now you can use your telescope! You must slide the sliding tubes back and forth slowly until the object you are looking at comes into focus.

Telescope Stand

After using your telescope a while, you may discover that a stand to hold the telescope steady is a good idea. Here is an easy one to make.

What you need:
tall cardboard box, a meter or more high
flathead bolt with nut
8 cm-by-30 cm strip of file folder
pushpins or paper punch
nail

1. Wrap the strip of file folder around the telescope's center. Tape the strip along the seam, but keep it just loose enough to slide it off the telescope. This will be the telescope's "cradle."

2. Slide the cradle off the telescope and punch a hole anywhere in the center of the cradle's side (use a paper punch or a pushpin). Enlarge the hole with a nail if necessary, until the bolt can slide through the hole.

3. Stick the bolt through the cradle from the inside, with the flathead end of the bolt resting on the inside of the cradle. Slide the cradle back on the telescope.

4. Make a hole in the side of the cardboard box, near the top of the box. Stick the bolt through the hole and fasten the nut onto the bolt from inside the box. The bolt acts as a pivot to allow the telescope to tilt up and down. To swing the telescope sideways, just rotate the whole box.

Alternative: If someone you know has a camera tripod, you can probably invent a way to attach your telescope to the tripod head.

Never look at the sun through this or any telescope!

Perseid meteor shower occurs every August 12 — a meteor a minute.

Arizona crater, caused by a meteor 25 meters wide, traveling 5,400 km/hour.

tail of gases remains straight

dust tail curves in solar wind

comet nucleus within coma

Shooters

"Shooting stars" aren't really stars at all, but meteors.

However, before they become meteors, they are known as meteoroids. Meteoroids are small pieces of natural debris or bits of comets that travel through space. Most are no bigger than a grain of sand.

There is no atmosphere in space, and, therefore, there is no friction. But Earth's atmosphere is thick with air molecules. When meteoroids enter Earth's atmosphere they blaze, and then they are called meteors. Meteors can be traveling more than 25,000 miles per hour when they enter our atmosphere. They heat up and burn fiercely when they crash into air molecules (that is why the space shuttles have heat-resistant panels on their outer surface for re-entry into the atmosphere). Any two materials or surfaces, when rubbed together, will generate friction and heat up. Rub your hands together really fast and feel what happens.

When very large meteors don't burn completely and end up smashing into Earth, they are called meteorites. Some meteorites are so big (up to several tons) that they destroy wide areas of Earth's surface and carve out craters. These larger meteorites explode at or near Earth's surface because of friction and the pressure of Earth's atmosphere. This happened in Siberia in 1908 when a meteorite caused the Tunguska explosion. Scientists believe the Tunguska meteorite (estimated to be 200 feet wide) exploded with the power equivalent to 20 million tons of TNT just before reaching the surface of Earth. It flattened at least 40,000 trees over a 772-square-mile area!

Some 50,000 years ago an even bigger meteorite actually landed in what is now the state of Arizona and gouged out a crater 4,000 feet across and almost 600 feet deep!

The moon's surface is also pocked with these enormous "impact craters." You can see them with your telescope or binoculars.

Comets

Comets are often thought of as red-hot cosmic balls with long flaming tails. They are really clumps of natural space debris—dust, rock, ice crystals, and gas—and not hot at all.

The head of a comet consists of a core or a nucleus one to ten miles in diameter that is surrounded by a vast cloud of dust and gas called a *coma*. Nuclei of comets are created when space debris collides and fuses together. Some comets may be chunks of planets, or leftovers from the big bang! (See page 40.) The comet's tail extends from the head and is also composed of gas and dust.

When a comet begins to approach the sun, the outer layers of its nucleus start to vaporize. Dust and gas string out behind the comet and form a tail that reflects brightly in the sun's light. Comet tails can stretch for millions of miles as they near the sun.

Because the sun produces a constant stream of excited atoms and light called solar winds, comet tails are *always* pushed away from the sun. When comets are approaching the sun, their tails are behind their heads. But when comets complete their approach, and speed away from the sun, their tails are in front!

Comets weave through the planets on long oval orbits around the sun. The length of their orbits determines how frequently comets can be seen. Some vagabond comets have "open orbits." They appear once, bend around the sun, then arc off into space, never to return. Some smaller comets vaporize completely, but the larger ones will keep returning for hundreds or even thousands of years as they orbit the sun.

The Big Bang

How was the universe created, and how big is it? Does space ever end? You may be asking these questions your whole life, because astronomers don't really know the answers.

There are many theories about how the universe was formed. Most religions maintain that their god (or gods) created the universe and all life, but most astronomers believe the universe began with a big bang about 15 billion years ago.

The big bang theory suggests that all matter, and eventually all life, was generated with an enormous superheated explosion of energy from a single point of dense celestial material. This blast created the universe's two original elements: hydrogen and helium. Carbon and oxygen (which help make you) were produced in stars that were formed after the big bang.

Sounds crazy? Maybe, but astronomers, using special devices called radio telescopes (they measure radio waves), can still detect a "cosmic wave" they believe was created by the big bang. And, they have proven that all the galaxies in the universe are zooming away from each other at great speeds. The universe is still expanding!

A Googol of Galaxies

There are basically two types of galaxies: flat, disk-shaped masses of stars called spiral galaxies, like ours, and egg- or cigar-shaped elliptical galaxies.

Our solar system is part of our vastly larger spiral galaxy that consists of an estimated 400 billion stars. Each star is a sun in its own right. Astronomers believe there could be over 100 billion galaxies in the universe. There might even be a *googol* of galaxies! A googol is 1 followed by 100 zeros. Are you exhausted just thinking about how many that is? If not, then consider this: each one of those galaxies probably contains a minimum of 100 million stars. Are you exhausted now?

Galactic Years and Light Speed

A galactic year is how long it takes our solar system to completely orbit the center of our galaxy. (Remember, we are situated partway out toward the edge of our spiral galaxy.) How long do you think it takes us to orbit? Forty-five minutes, two months, ten years? Try 225 million years. One galactic year ago, dinosaurs roamed the earth.

The universe is so enormous that trying to measure it in millions of miles would be impractical. There would be too many millions (and zeros) to keep track of. So space distances are usually measured in light-years: the distance light travels in a year.

Light travels at 186,000 miles per second. This works out to about 11 million miles a minute and 6 trillion miles a year (that's 6 followed by 12 zeros). The sun's light takes about 8½ minutes to reach us.

What about the light from Sirius in the Big Dog constellation, the brightest star in our sky? It takes about 8.8 years to reach us! If the distance between Earth and the sun—one astronomical unit (AU)—was reduced to 1 inch, Sirius would be located more than 9 miles away.

If the universe was reduced to this same scale, the stars would be like small grains of floating sand, separated by about a mile of empty space.

From your perspective on Earth, the constellations you see look like groupings of stars that are located close to each other. Wrong! For example, two of the stars in the Big Dipper's handle, Alcor and Mizar, appear very close to each other. But Mizar is 78 light-years away from us, and Alcor is another 120 light-years beyond Mizar!

There is a *lot* of space in space. Astronomers know there is a lot of empty space up there, but they still don't know how big the universe really is.

Deep Darkness

Darkness is everywhere in the vast emptiness of space. But how can that be when there are so many stars, like our sun, sending light out into space all the time?

The only time we see light in space is when it reaches our eyes *directly* from stars, or is *reflected* off of objects like planets, the moon, and satellites. Since there is so much space in space, and not many objects to reflect light, darkness prevails. The light from all of those stars travels deeper and deeper into space, but only a small fraction of it ever reaches us.

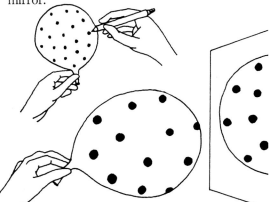

Dawn

As your body prepares to wake in the still hours of dawn, the stars overhead are the ones that will be overhead at dusk six months from now. The outside air temperature drops to its lowest point just before sunrise, squeezing moisture from the air and forming dew. Watery diamonds dangle from spiderwebs. Mice sip drops from grass-blade fountains and leaf-tip cups. Frogs and salamanders glisten as they hunt, knowing that tasty earthworms emerge from their subterranean world at dawn to squirm on the damp soil.

The night is about to end, but many creatures linger in the cool half-light, serenaded by a morning chorus of birds. Nightshift creatures press their final set of tracks into the moist earth, and the curtain falls on your last dream of the night. Good morning.

Rise and Shine

Even if a grown-up doesn't shake you by the shoulder to wake you up in the morning, or the snooze-alarm on your clock is broken, and even if your dog forgets to give you a big wet kiss, you'd still wake up. How does your body know when to rise and shine? It's that old team again—your biological clock, circadian rhythm, and neurotransmitters produced by your brain.

Before waking, your brain produces different neurotransmitters (wake-up juices) that overpower the neurotransmitters that helped you sleep. These "wake-up juices" tell your brain and body to begin a new day. Throughout the day these chemicals slowly "drip" into your body and keep you awake. By bedtime, more of the "sleeping potion" is produced than the "wake-up juices" and you get sleepy.

Dreams

You may believe you don't dream. But scientists have proven that *everyone* dreams at least a thousand times a year, or about three times a night. The most vivid dreams occur during REM sleep, which you enter three or four times nightly.

You may think you don't dream because you can't remember your dreams. That takes practice. Usually you only remember dreams if you wake up immediately after you have had one. Even then, dreams tend to slip away quickly from memory, a phenomenon called *oneirolysis*.

Dream Diary

It takes practice to remember your dreams. Here is how to make it a little easier:

What you need:

paper
pen or pencil
tape recorder (optional)
flashlight or lamp

1. Place your pen and paper next to your bed. If you can't turn on a lamp in the middle of the night, have a small flashlight handy. Some pens come with their own light.

2. Climb into bed and relax. Before you fall asleep, remind yourself that you are going to remember your dreams. Think about dreaming, and how you will record your dreams when you wake. (Don't laugh! This really works.)

3. If you wake during the night, try not to go back to sleep right away. Instead, record any dream you can remember—even a piece of one. If you can recall even one small part, you may suddenly remember more.

4. If you don't wake in the middle of the night, then record your last dream as soon as you wake in the morning. You'll be surprised how much you will remember.

Record *everything* about your dreams—sensations, emotions, colors, and dialogue. Don't worry about what your dreams mean while you're recording them. You can do that later. If you are using a tape recorder, transcribe your dreams onto paper during the day.

Signs of Life

Put on a sweater and step outside. While you slept, nightshift creatures were leaving their marks in your neighborhood. Most folks won't notice these signs. But you can. Here is where the neighbor's cat chased a field mouse; you can see the tracks in that damp patch of dirt. There is a frayed end of a twig where a deer nibbled a nighttime snack. The gray and black hairs that are stuck to the bottom of the fence tell you a raccoon crawled under it last night. And that black, shiny lump at the edge of the garden was left by a toad, who is somewhere in a damp corner, settling down for the day.

If you look carefully and slowly, the signs of the night's adventures are all around you. Here are some things you can look for. But first, some tracking terminology.

Tracking

The stride and print size of a species will vary a little, just as the way people walk and the size of their feet aren't all the same. Also, prints look different when pressed into snow, sand, mud, or dust.

Print: the impression made by one foot
Track: a series of prints
Straddle: the width of the track
Stride: the distance between prints
Leap: the distance between sets of prints made by hoppers or bounders
Straight-line Walkers. If the track makes a straight line, and the animal is placing its hind feet almost exactly into the print made by the front feet, then it is probably a member of the dog or cat family. Animals with hoofs, like deer, are also straight-line walkers.

Zigzaggers. If prints form a zigzag track—they don't cover each other—and the straddle is wide, then heavy-set creatures, such as raccoons, skunks, and opossums, have been prowling nearby.

Bounders. If regularly spaced pairs or groups of prints make up the track, it was probably made by a creature in the weasel family or a vole.

Deer, with no upper front teeth, pull and rip leaves and twigs.

Rabbits clip twigs neatly between their upper and lower incisors.

— Who left the crayfish shells?

scat

It was black and shiny. Under the magnifying glass we saw it was almost all beetle parts! Skunk?

Leapers and Hoppers. Tracks that consist of sets of two small prints and two large prints tell you a rabbit or some other rodent dashed by. They land on both front feet, then they swing their hind feet ahead of their front ones.

Sliders and Crawlers. Who needs furry feet or hooves to make tracks? All creatures, including frogs, lizards, snakes, and crickets, leave tracks.

More Clues

Scat. Scat is a general term for animal droppings, and it's a good sign of what animals are around and what they're eating. If it's packed with fur, bones, and feathers, it probably came from a creature in the dog, cat, or weasel family. If it looks like pellets of sawdust or dry plant material, deer, rabbits, or porcupines may have visited last night.

Wildlife biologists *always* collect scat, and there are even specialists in scatology (the study of scat). Scat is usually dry and harmless to handle. But if it bothers you to pick up scat, use a twig or a trowel. Don't be squirmy—become a scatologist! Just be sure to wash your hands when you've finished your examinations.

Twigs, Limbs, and Bones. Many nocturnal creatures chew on twigs, limbs, and bones for food and to sharpen their teeth. They also leave "prints" with their teeth.

Miniature gnaw marks on pieces of wood or bone mean mice have been working. Rabbit marks are less than ⅛ inch wide. Large chew marks on trunks or limbs, ⅛ inch and wider, are the work of beavers or porcupines. If the marks are high on a tree, they're the work of porcupines. Beavers can't climb. Beavers work at the base of small trees and often eat completely through them. Porcupines also chew bones.

Twig ends that are severed close to the ground with one or more sharp cuts may be the work of rabbits. Ragged twig ends higher up have most likely been chewed by deer. If the tips of fallen antlers are chewed and ragged, then you can tell that deer have been chewing them. Seems strange, but deer eat the antlers of other deer sometimes, even when they are still attached!

Tree trunks are used by bears and mountain lions for scratching and by deer for rubbing the velvet off their antlers.

To learn more about tracks, scat, twigs, limbs, and bones, look for: *A Field Guide to Animal Tracks*, by Olaus J. Murie.

Collecting Prints

Now that you know how to recognize some tracks, start a nightwatch creature print collection.

What you need:
plaster of paris or similar material
medium-sized can
water
stirring stick
watch
heavy paper (optional)

The best prints to preserve are those left in dirt, firm mud, or moist sand. Look for prints around your house, apartment, or in a nearby park. When you find one you want to collect:

1. Clear away loose dirt or leaves that might stick to your casting.
2. Mix some plaster with water to make it runny enough to pour easily. It should be the consistency of thick pancake batter.
3. Pour the plaster "batter" into the print so it spills over the sides and covers the entire print.
4. Don't touch your cast until the plaster has set (about ten minutes). Dig around the print and lift it out gently. Let it dry for one day, then rinse off the remaining dirt under running water. An old toothbrush or vegetable brush works fine as a scrubber.

If the print is on a slope or isn't very deep, you can build a "collar" around the print to hold the plaster better. Pile a firm ring of dirt around the print, or place a 2-inch ring of heavy paper around it. If you are using heavy paper, press snugly against the ground so the plaster doesn't ooze out at the bottom.

Now, who made that track?

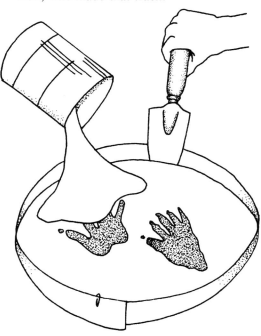

Track Spot

You can make your own print collection spot, if you can't find a good place to hunt for tracks.

After getting permission, scrape out a dirt or sand area outside about 4 feet by 4 feet. Remove all weeds and large stones. Loosen the soil then smooth it out with a board. Sprinkle it down with water (*don't* make a mud bath). Place some scraps (bread, fruit, a chunk of tuna fish) in the center. In the morning, see who was walking around last night.

The Morning Chorus

robin

sparrow

wren

mockingbird

robin sparrow mockingbird

An hour before you see *any* light on the horizon, birds are already singing outside your window. Mockingbirds and some other birds sing all night in warm weather. By the early light of dawn, almost every daytime bird has joined in to create the sweet sounds of the morning chorus.

Early philosophers and naturalists thought birds sang in the early morning to celebrate dawn's beauty. Although this explanation sounds nice, modern scientists who study birds, *ornithologists*, believe birds sing at dawn to reclaim their territory.

The morning chorus is especially loud during the spring and summer nesting season. Competition is fierce during this period for mates, nesting territory, and food.

Male birds stake out a territory at the beginning of nesting season. When not eating or mating during the day, they fly the border of their territory, stopping to sing at prominent trees and bushes.

These birds have learned that it is safer to sing loudly all day, defending territory, than it is to fight over males. Where territories of the same species are close to each other, males sometimes sing just a few feet apart, without ever attacking each other.

After the nesting season, territories are no longer defended, and the morning songs quiet down. In winter, many birds have migrated south, and those that stay sing only a little at dawn.

Early Birds Catch the Light

Just like you and other animals, birds have circadian rhythms or biological clocks. That means their biological functions are set on a 24-hour schedule. So they know when it is time to wake up and sing in the morning.

Also, birds can detect the faint rays of the rising sun an hour or more before you can, even if you use binoculars! That's because their eyes have more rods and cones than you do and are much more sensitive to light. In dim light, they see more clearly than you do. When there is a bright moon at dawn, birds begin singing even earlier. When it is cloudy and overcast, they start singing later.

Early Risers

Here are some of the first birds you'll hear singing, besides those crowing roosters.

Robin

The loud, liquid song of the robin (*Turdus migratorius*) can be heard across the U.S. It sounds like a bouncing *cheerily cheer-up cheerio*, repeated over and over for several minutes. After singing, robins can be seen on lawns and in fields, searching for worms, snails, berries, and fruit.

Cardinal

Cardinals (*Cardinalis cardinalis*) live in the Southwest and central and eastern U.S., and they eat seeds, insects, and fruit. Their song can vary but includes refrains like *cue cue cue* and *cheer cheer cheer* and *purty purty purty* as well as many whistles.

Song Sparrow

This bird (*Melospiza melodia*) sings across the U.S., and its typical song consists of three or four short, clear notes followed by a buzzy *tow-wee*, then a tapering *trill*. When the song sparrow sings, it throws back its head and its entire body shakes.

cardinal

towhee

wren towhee cardinal

House Wren

This energetic little bird's scientific name, *Troglodytes aedon*, means "the cave-dwelling nightingale." It nests in tree holes ("caves") everywhere in the U.S. Its cascading bubbling song is as beautiful as that of Europe's famous nightingale. When not singing, the house wren can be seen jumping around in bushes and trees, searching for insects.

Mockingbird

This bird's scientific name, *Mimus polyglottos*, means the "multilingual mimicker." The mockingbird's song is a mixture of original sounds and mocked or borrowed songs. It can imitate other birds, creaking gates, musical instruments, and barking dogs. During the spring, males often sing all day *and* night almost everywhere in the U.S.

Rufous-sided Towhee

The rufous-sided towhee's scientific name, *Pipilo erythrophthalmus*, means the "red-eyed chirper." In addition to its beautiful black, white, and orange-red (rufous) plumage, it has bright red eyes. Its short call is a slurred *chewink*, and another call is a long, drawn-out *chweeeeee*. Its song almost sounds like it is saying "drink-your-tea!"

Local Singers

What you need:
local newspaper
alarm clock
watch
warm clothes
nightwatch journal and pen
flashlight

1. Look in your newspaper's weather section for the time of sunrise the next day. Let's say it is 6:30 A.M. Set your alarm for one hour and 15 minutes before sunrise, 5:15 A.M.

2. Before you go to sleep, take a page from your nightwatch journal and write 5:30 A.M., 5:40, 5:50, and so on until 6:30 down the left-hand column.

3. When your alarm goes off in the morning, you have 15 minutes to put on your warm clothes and your watch, grab your journal, pen, and flashlight, and step outside. Get comfortable, because you aren't going to move until sunrise.

Okay. Every ten minutes, write down how many birds you hear. (Look at your watch with the flashlight; the light won't affect your ears!)

If you do this every few weeks for a year, you'll have an excellent record of what morning chorus birds have visited your yard.

To learn your bird calls, contact your local library or Audubon Society and ask if they have bird song records, tapes, or videos that you can borrow or buy. Look for: *A Field Guide to Bird Songs*, *The Peterson Field Guide Series* (record, Western and Eastern U.S. editions), or *Audubon Society's Videoguide to the Birds of North America*.

Greenpatch Kid

He Is Serious About His Birds

Cooper Scollan is a lot like the rest of his teammates on the Carmel High School tennis team. The only difference is that between sets, Cooper talks with the great horned owl that roosts in an oak tree near the court. "It's great," says Cooper. "I just call up there—*hoo, hoo-oo, hoo, hoo*—and he calls back."

Cooper takes his interest in owls off the court, too. Since he was introduced to owls and birdwatching when he was ten years old, Cooper has gone out at night "owling" more times than he can remember. He has seen 13 owl species in North America, and a couple more in Costa Rica and the Hawaiian Islands.

At first his parents thought Cooper was crazy because he liked to venture out in the middle of the night and hoot into trees. But soon they were joining Cooper on his owling adventures. Cooper encouraged them to stay up until midnight, or to get up at 3 A.M., go outside, call for owls, and patiently wait. "I am trying to learn all my owl calls," says the young owler. "But for now I play tapes to call owls if I don't know their calls. I even recorded the live call of a spotted owl once with a friend's equipment. Then we played it back, and a spotted flew real close to investigate us."

All this practice and patience (which Cooper just calls fun) pays off. Cooper once saw six owls in a single night in Carmel Valley. Although Cooper still spends a lot of time playing tennis, he is also serious about his birds. "I've seen over 500 bird species in six years. I hope to go to college and study ornithology."

Resources

Goatsuckers and Owls

To get an idea of what goatsuckers and owls look and sound like, ask if your local library has the Audubon Society's Video Guide to the Birds of North America: III. If they don't have it, and you want to order a copy, call or write: Audubon Society's Video Guide to the Birds of North America: III; P.O. Box 460; Clinton, TN 37716-0460; 1-800-846-0123; $29.95 (plus $5.00 handling).

You can also look for the following field guide book to get you on your way: *Birds of North America*, 1983, National Geographic Society, Washington, D.C.

Insects and Spiders

The Young Entomologists Society is a good organization for amateur bug fanatics. They have three publications for young entomologists. Also, there are plenty of great books that can help you learn more about these fascinating creatures.

Young Entomologists Society (YES); 1915 Peggy Pl.; Lansing, MI 48910; 517-887-0499; annual dues: $5.00.

YES Publications: *Insect World*, $8.00/year. (Articles for elementary school age kids.) *YES Quarterly*, $12.00/year. (More serious articles for teenagers written by fellow YES members.) *Flea Market*, $7.00/year. (Classified ads listing insects to buy or trade, insect-catching equipment, books, and events.)

If reading about insects and spiders gets you so excited that you want to start collecting them, then you should call the Carolina Biological Supply Company in North Carolina or its West Coast office in Oregon (both places carry the exact same items). You can order everything—live moths, ants, mantids, a variety of cocoons, and even cockroaches! They also sell mounted (dead) moths and other nighttime insects. Their 1,300-page catalog costs $17.95, *but* don't worry; their offices maintain toll-free telephone numbers that are staffed by people who will take orders from you even if you don't have a catalog. Plus, many science and biology teachers have copies of the catalog on hand (ask yours). If you live on the East Coast, call the company in North Carolina; if you live on the West Coast, call Oregon; if you live in Kansas, toss a coin.

Carolina Biological Supply Company; 2700 York Rd.; Burlington, NC 27215; 1-800-334-5551.

Powell Labs; Division of Carolina Biological Supply Company; P.O. Box 187; Gladstone, OR 97027; 1-800-547-1733.

Bats

To find out more about bats, and what you can do to help them, write: Bat Conservation International; P.O. Box 162603; Austin, TX 78716-2603; 512-327-9721; annual dues: $25.00/year. With membership you receive their quarterly newsletter *BATS*, and their merchandise catalog.

While you are waiting for a reply from Bat Conservation International, look for this book in your library: *America's Neighborhood Bats* by Merlin D. Tuttle, Austin: University of Texas Press, 1988.

Endangered Species

If you want to find out more about endangered species, write or call the U.S. Fish and Wildlife Service's Publication Unit, and ask them for their publication on endangered and threatened wildlife and plants, or ask them a question about a specific species. They have numerous free brochures on individual species and the programs to help save them. You can also contact the Endangered Species Coalition and your Fish and Game Department in your state capital to find out what type of information they have.

U.S. Fish and Wildlife Service; Publications Unit; 4401 N. Fairfax Dr.; Mail Stop 130 Webb; Arlington, VA 22203; 703-358-1711.

Endangered Species Coalition; c/o National Audubon Society; 666 Pennsylvania Ave., SE; Washington, DC 20003.

Adopt-a-Species Program

If you live in California or New Mexico, find out about the great "Adopt-a-Species Program" sponsored by the National Audubon Society to help save endangered species and their habitat. You must join this program as a group, and there is an annual prize and award ceremony for the contestants.

California: National Audubon Society; Richardson Bay Audubon Center; 376 Greenwood Beach Rd.; Tiburon, CA 94942; 415-388-2524.

New Mexico: National Audubon Society; Randall Davey Audubon Center; P.O. Box 9314; Santa Fe, NM 87504; 505-983-4609.

Astronomy and Spacelink

The Astronomical Society of the Pacific is for young astronomers and star-gazing buffs around the world. Give them a call, or write them, and they will send you membership information and a free issue of their newsletter. You can also call your local planetarium, or the astronomy department at a nearby college, and ask them questions.

Astronomical Society of the Pacific; 390 Ashton Ave.; San Francisco, CA 94112; 415-337-1100; annual dues: $25.00. With membership you will receive *Mercury Magazine* (6 times a year), a monthly sky calendar, and a merchandise catalog that includes stuff such as computer software for astronomy, videos, posters, slide sets, and books.

For questions about the U.S. space program and general astronomy, the National Aeronautics and Space Administration (NASA) operates a program called Spacelink out of Huntsfield, Alabama. You connect with Spacelink via a computer modem. Spacelink's modem number is: 205 895 0028; its Internet address is: spacelink.msfc.nasa.gov. If your grown-up, a friend, your school, or your local natural history museum has a modem or belongs to an Internet, you can hook up with Spacelink to access all sorts of free information, like 5,000 articles and over 2,000 images. And, if you have a specific question you can't find the answer to, such as "Where is NASA's closest Teaching Resource Center?" you can leave it on Spacelink, and someone at NASA will answer you within 24 hours!

Here are some great books to help you learn more about the night sky: *Astronomy Today* by Eric Chaisson and Steve McMillan, New York: Prentice-Hall, 1992. *Astronomy for Every Kid* by Janice Pratt VanCleave, New York: John Wiley & Sons, 1991. *The Audubon Society Field Guide to the Night Sky* by Mark R. Chartrand, New York: Alfred A. Knopf, 1991. *The Night Sky Book* by Jamie Jobb, Boston: Little, Brown and Company, 1977. *The Stars* by H. A. Rey, Boston: Houghton Mifflin Company, 1975. *Seeing the Sky: 100 Projects, Activities & Explorations in Astronomy* by Fred Schaaf, New York: John Wiley & Sons, 1990.

Acknowledgments

The author received help from many people. Alan Gould and the Lawrence Hall of Science (U.C. Berkeley) offered their telescope plan, and Alan helped with night sky facts. The Astronomical Society of the Pacific provided information for the moon phase and lunar eclipse charts. Meryl Sundove and Bill Bixby of the Richardson Bay Audubon Center helped with natural history topics, and Bat Conservation International personnel checked all bat facts. Libby Wilkinson, researcher and model firefly maker *extraordinaire*, was a key idea person. Dr. Isaac Silberman helped with the physiology of sleeping and waking, and the Mill Valley Library staff was informative and encouraging throughout.

Scientific Classifications

Scientists have identified almost two million plants and animals. And people are discovering more every day!

To keep everything straight, scientists use a system that divides animals, plants, and other creatures into groups, depending upon how they are built. Organisms with similar structures are put together in one group, while those with very different structures go into other groups.

Scientists use this system to divide and subdivide living things into smaller and smaller groups depending upon how much alike they are. If two animals are identical down to the species (the smallest group), they are very closely related. If two animals are in different phyla (large groups), they are quite different from each other.

Here are the different divisions, and how you fit into the scheme of things: There are five **kingdoms**, the broadest classification. These include plants, animals, fungi (mushrooms), protists (protozoa and algae), and monera (bacteria). Humans are animals so you belong in that group.

The animal kingdom is divided into many different **phyla** (the singular is **phylum**). Your phylum is *Chordata*, and your **subphylum** (a smaller group within a phylum) is *Vertebrata* because you have a backbone.

Each phylum is divided into **classes**. Your class is *Mammalia*. All mammals are warm-blooded and somewhat hairy, with young that feed on the female's milk. Do you still fit?

Each class is divided into **orders**. Your order is *Primata*. All primates have flexible, five-fingered hands and feet. Are you still with me?

Your **family**, the next smaller group, is *Hominidae*. Hominids include all of the two-legged primates. Do you usually walk on two legs? Good, you're correctly classified.

The next subgroup is the **genus**. Your genus is *Homo*—a group that includes both modern and extinct groups of humans.

The **species** is the smallest group. It consists of animals with very similar structures that breed to produce offspring. Modern humans are alone in this species identified as *Homo sapiens*. You're not extinct, so I think you qualify.

Glossary

amphibian any animal such as a frog, toad, or newt whose young have gills and live in water and whose adults have lungs and live on land.

anticoagulant any substance that slows the clotting of blood.

Arachnid a member of the class Arachnida. Arachnids have segmented bodies divided into two parts and have four pairs of legs.

astronomical unit (AU) a unit of measurement used in astronomy equal to the average distance between Earth and the sun, about 93 million miles.

auroras long, wavy bands of light that happen around the North and South Poles and are caused by solar winds hitting Earth's magnetic field. If you go to Alaska or northern Canada you can see the aurora borealis (the northern lights).

axis the line between the North and South Poles around which Earth rotates.

binary stars twin stars that, instead of shining alone like our sun, revolve together around one spot in space.

biological clock what determines when you wake up and go to sleep. It is based on a 24-hour cycle.

bioluminescence the glow of light that comes from a living creature, such as a firefly.

carnivorous eating only animals.

celestial of or relating to the sky or universe. The planets and the stars are called celestial bodies.

chelicerae fanglike structures that spiders use to eat their prey.

chemoreceptors special cells in your nose and mouth that are sensitive to tiny chemical molecules in scents and food. These are what allow you to smell and taste.

Chiroptera the order of mammals (the name means "hand-wing") that includes bats.

circadian rhythm a 24-hour cycle.

circumpolar circumpolar stars revolve around the North Star and are always visible in the night sky. Some circumpolar constellations are Cassiopeia, Draco, and the Big Dipper.

cocoon the pupa of a moth.

coma the vast cloud of dust and gas that surrounds a comet's nucleus.

comet a clump of natural space debris—dust, rock, ice crystals, and gas—that orbits the sun.

compound eyes insect eyes made of many facets, each of which sense movement and light. They create a blurry image but are good at sensing motion.

cones the parts of the eye that help distinguish details.

constellation one of 88 groups of stars that suggest a picture. Seeing a constellation in the sky is like figuring out a connect-the-dots drawing without using a pencil.

cribellum a special spinning organ that cribellate spiders have to produce ultrafine silk for their webs.

diurnal active during the day.

echolocation how a bat determines what and where something is. When bats fly, they send out a series of very high clicks. The sound of these clicks bounces off of animals and objects back to the bat.

eclipse the total or partial obscuring of one celestial body by another.

equinox a time when the day and night are of equal length (12 hours each). There are two equinoxes each year—the vernal in March and the autumnal in September.

facet a lenslike division of an insect's compound eye.

fibroin the strong liquid substance that makes up the fibers of spider silk.

galactic year how long it takes our solar system to completely orbit the center of the galaxy. One galactic year is approximately 225 million Earth years.

galaxy a group of stars. There are two kinds of galaxies: spiral (like ours) and elliptical.

larva in the development from egg to adult, the larva is an intermediate form that is unlike the adult. The transformation from egg to adult is called metamorphosis. Some larvae and their adults are: tadpoles and frogs, caterpillars and moths, maggots and flies.

light-year a unit for measuring space equal to the distance light travels in one year—about 6 trillion miles (6,000,000,000,000 miles).

luciferin the pigment in a firefly's abdomen that produces a blue-green light when combined with oxygen.

marsupial a mammal that gives birth to tiny young who crawl into a pouch on their mother's belly, where they continue to develop. Opossums and kangaroos are marsupials.

meteor a meteoroid (small pieces of debris) that has entered Earth's atmosphere. Because of the friction that is caused by their entry, meteors usually burn up before they hit Earth. Meteors are sometimes called shooting stars and can be seen on clear, moonless nights.

meteorite a large meteor that doesn't burn up when it hits Earth's atmosphere. Meteorites crash into Earth and very large ones leave craters at the point of impact.

meteoroids small pieces of natural debris or bits of comets that travel through space.

nebula a vast cloud of dust and gas in space.

neurotransmitter a chemical that carries signals between nerve cells.

nocturnal active during the night.

omnivorous eating both plants and animals.

oneirolysis when your dreams slip quickly from your memory.

orbit to revolve in a circular path around another object. The path itself is also called an orbit.

ornithologist a person who studies birds.

pellet the little ball an owl coughs up that is made of bones and fur left over from its meal.

phototaxis when an animal such as a moth arranges its position according to a light source like the moon or your porch light.

polarized light light that has been filtered so that its waves have a simple arrangement.

pollinator something that carries the pollen from the male part of a flower to the female part. Some important pollinators are bees, bats, moths, butterflies, and the wind.

prehensile adapted for grabbing by wrapping around something. Opossums and monkeys have prehensile tails.

proboscis a slender, tubular feeding and sucking mouthpart of some insects such as moths, flies, mosquitoes, and butterflies.

pupate to change from a larva into an adult insect.

rapid eye movement (REM) this fluttering of your eyes happens while you are in the REM phase of sleep. Your fingers and toes might also twitch during this time.

rods the parts of the eye that absorb light.

rut the season during the winter when deer mate.

satellite a man-made object that is designed to orbit Earth. Satellites are used to monitor things like the weather or to transmit radio waves or television signals.

scat animal droppings.

scientific name see Scientific Classifications, p. 46.

simple eye an eye that is used to tell the difference between light and dark. Spiders and crickets both have simple eyes.

spigots the tiny openings on a spider's abdomen through which it pulls its silk.

tapetum the shiny membrane behind a nocturnal animal's layer of rods and cones. At night, the tapetum reflects weak light back through the eye. By using the light twice, the animal sees better in the dark.

ultrasonic sounds that are so high-pitched humans cannot hear them.

ultraviolet light light is both visible and nonvisible energy that travels in waves. Different kinds of light are categorized by the length of their wave. Ultraviolet light, the light that causes suntans and sunburns, is not visible to humans because its wavelength is too short.

variable stars stars whose light does not remain constant like our sun's. Instead, their light varies or changes during a certain period of time.

vibrissae stiff hairs that are usually located near a mammal's or bird's mouth and are very sensitive organs of touch. Owls, goatsuckers, and cats have vibrissae.

Index

The Greenpatch Kids Want You!

All over the world, this very minute, kids just like you are working to make the earth a safe place for all living things. There is a lot to do. You and your friends can help. If you do, you will be joining hundreds and thousands of kids everywhere. Here are some ways you can get started:

1. Join the Greenpatch Kids.

The Greenpatch Kids is an alliance of young people who want to learn about the environment and how to protect it. Anyone can join. If your copy of this book includes a mail-back card, complete the form with your name and address, and send it in. (Don't forget a stamp.) If there isn't a card in your book, write your name, address, age, and school on a piece of paper, put it in an envelope, and send it to the address below. You will receive a Greenpatch membership card and a free copy of the *Greenpatch News*, which is full of ideas for projects and will tell you what other kids are doing. Write to:

Greenpatch Kids
Harcourt Brace Children's Books
525 B Street, Suite 1900
San Diego, CA 92101

2. Start a Greenpatch Kids group.

Governments and big environmental groups can't always work in your neighborhood, but you and your friends sure can! All you need is an adult sponsor, some friends, and a plan.

Do a neighborhood bio-survey. What animals and plants live there? Are any of them endangered? What can you do to protect them? Start a pollution watch. The health of our earth *starts in your neighborhood*.

3. Tell us about your project.

The people who made this book and Greenpatch Kids everywhere want to know what you are doing. Your idea might be just what someone else needs. If you have a project that works, send us a description. Be sure to include your name, address, age, and telephone number, in case we need to contact you for more information.

4. Contact and work with other groups.

To get help for your project, or to find out what to do in your neighborhood, contact other groups. The largest environmental group for young people is *Kids for Saving Earth*. It costs $7 to join (or $15 for your group), but they will send you a free information pack if you write or call them. Ask them if there is already a KSE group in your town. Write *Kids for Saving Earth*, P.O. Box 47247, Plymouth, MN 55447, or phone 612-525-0002.